# Skydiving
# with Jesus

# Skydiving
# with Jesus

*A Journey from Fear to Faith*

Chad Brown and Josh Knipple

ISBN: 1979733597
ISBN-13: 9781979733595
Library of Congress Control Number: 2017918335
CreateSpace Independent Publishing Platform
North Charleston, South Carolina

# About the Author

## Chad Brown

Chad Brown is an evangelist and motivational speaker. Chad also works with the co-author of this book, Josh Knipple, as a local missionary based out of Crucified Church in Johnstown, PA. Our desire is to see people set on fire with the love of Jesus. We want to see people set free from the things of this world that can entangle us all. Chads' story proves that God can transform a life of addiction, suicidal thoughts, and depression. God can give us freedom from ourselves, so we live with passion for the one who spoke the universe into existence.

Chad's first love in ministry is to see people not just meet, but follow Jesus. "I believe we exist to bring glory to this amazing creator" he says. "Too many of us have walked aimlessly around in this life without knowing our identity in Jesus. We aim to guide people into that truth and experience and insane life filled with Him". To this end, Chad is traveling around teaching the Bible and motivating people to live all out, taking it one day at a time for the King.

Chad has earned an undergraduate degree from Liberty University in Religion, and a Masters degree in Theological Studies from Liberty. He is currently working on a second Master's degree in Global Studies from L.U. Prior to his current traveling ministry, he has served as a youth pastor and held a position as Bible/Apologetics teacher at a High School in Maryland.

Chad and his wife, Leah, are Texas natives who have made their home in Johnstown, Pa. They feel called to that area which has seen a lot of brokenness, but with the power of the Holy Spirit there are incredible things taking place. Chad loves his God, family, surfing, the Lion King and rainy days.

**To find out more about what Chad is doing check out his website at www.chadmotivates.com. You can also connect with Chad on Facebook and Instagram @chadmotivates.**

## Josh Knipple

Josh Knipple is the founder of Crucified Ministries and the Senior Pastor at Crucified Church. He has been in full time ministry now for over ten years, speaking locally as well as internationally. The ministry began as a skate outreach and has now expanded into missions, homeless ministry, a traveling skate team, and everything in between.

His heart is truly just to see men and women living out their faith and seeing God as part of their everyday lives. He truly believes in Acts 1:8, "The spirit will come upon them with power, that they might be His witness." He believes this verse is true for all believers and wants to see others living with a passion.

Throughout his time in ministry he has gotten to share from major platforms at music festivals, yet his true heart is for the one on one conversations of everyday interaction and relationship. "Major speaking events are incredible to reach the masses, but I believe true change takes place being in the daily grind with people, seeing them in the good and the bad, the hurt and the joy."

Josh has his bachelor's degree from Liberty University in Religion with a focus on Youth Ministry.

He currently lives in Johnstown Pennsylvania with his wife Lindsey and 2 sons Silas and Eli. "We are starting to see our town changed for Jesus one family, one home at a time." If you can't seem to find Josh in town, go check the local mountain where he may be snowboarding with his family, or kayaking on the local lake. Honestly, just go outdoors, He isn't one to stay inside.

**To check out more of where Josh is, follow him on facebook @Crucifiedchurch or @challengetherordinary. Also you can follow his blog, eyes-ofachild.com**

"Chad has a phenomenal story, he has a heart for people, you gotta hear his story. I got a great story, but Chad's story is phenomenal and I believe will bring freedom to a lot of people. "
–Jeremy Anderson. Worldwide Motivational Speaker

"Love what you are doing, and you're always inspirational Mr. Knipple!"
-Josh Marburger. One Love Skate Outreach

"Chad blew me away with how he connects with teens, many came to know the Lord. Chad's message is outstanding and he has an incredible way of reaching the younger generation. Chad and Leah Brown truly have a servant's hIeart."
-Mark Witt. Director Teenquest Ranch

"I've known Josh for years. Through the time I have witnessed him living what you will read on these pages. True kindness shoots for the heart, Josh hits the bullseye."
-Eric Samuel Timm NoOneUnderground

"I absolutely love what you guys have done. Powerful stuff, and maybe even more important, practical."
-Ray Streets, The Journey Church

# Foreword

've had the privilege of knowing Chad and Josh over the years. It all started in classes at Liberty University. What is unique about those classes, is that those classes were youth ministry classes and the students in those classes were all about youth ministry. So while you are seeing these guys, maybe for the first time, I've been able to see their heart and enthusiasm for youth ministry germinate from classroom discussion and assignments, to hands-on, frontline ministries that are having a significant impact on teenagers. This is no ego-trip for these guys. They want to see teenagers reached for the Kingdom and they want to see teenagers reach *for* the Kingdom. This 31 day journey will help teenagers in their faith and you can be confident the authors bring a passion and commitment that is contagious.

-Dr. Steve Vandegriff- Liberty University

# A Few Thank You's

Josh: Thank you Mom and Dad for being the example you have been over the years. Dad for teaching me what grace is truly about and putting actions behind your words. You will always be the first to respond in a time of emergency and I cannot thank you enough for instilling that in me. Mom, for the love and kindness you show, you are the example of what it means to place others needs in front of your own. Travis, for the commitment you have made to missions, and for teaching me what it means to "step up or shut up." To my wife Lindsey, for being my encouragement, even on the days where I have wanted to throw in the towel, keeping me focused, and creating a place of refuge called our home. You have made sacrifices in our marriage that I can never repay you for. I love you! To my lil man Eli, you have truly taught me more about my faith in the last two years than I could have ever imagined. To Chad, for challenging me and partnering with me in the book to make faith practical. To all my friends over the years who have challenged me, pushed me, and not allowed me to live a mediocre life. All of you know who you are, and I hope and pray I have had the same impact on you. To Old Man Sam, who taught me to live a life that no one would believe if there weren't pictures. From partying with Elvis, to owning an olive oil company in Greece, to being a world record weightlifter, you has inspired me to live. Finally to my Savior himself Jesus Christ. A big thanks that you didn't design me to live a boring, sit on the couch life doing nothing, but created me with passion and a purpose. You did what I could never do no matter how tough I might like to think at times, you shed your blood and took on my sin, a weight I can't even fathom. So beyond saying Thank You I hope this book was a blessing to you.

Chad: This project is a product of how God has worked in my life.

Thank you to my wife for being on this journey with me and wanting to be married to someone as odd as I am. You and I have had a crazy ride and God is using our story to change others. Thank you for staying up late with me and giving me feedback. You're a hottie!!

Thank you to my parents who raised me in a home that pointed us toward the heart of God. My mom who has always tried to teach me about my identity in Jesus and my dad who pushed me to aim high and not to settle. This book is one of my B.H.A.G's.

Thank you to my kids for being ridiculously funny and giving me ideas. You guys are awesome!!

I want to thank Josh Knipple for being real with me since the first day I met him. Thank you for always asking me what God has been teaching me.... even though it was annoying for a while. You were my example of Christ in college. You were honest about flaws, failures and the insane GRACE of God. Thank you for introducing me to the real Jesus.

Thank you to my sister for putting up with me when we were younger. You continuously grow in Christ and it is an example to me and others. Thank you for being an example of Christ love when it wasn't easy. Our trip to McDonalds will never be forgotten.

Thank you Pastor Nissen for being an incredible man of God and showing us what it's like to be consistently in love with Jesus in an inconsistent world.

Thank you to Dr. Vandegriff for just being awesome!

Thank you D.W. for being a friend when I was at my lowest and I saw my end in sight. God used you brother! I might not be alive today if it wasn't for you.

Thank you to all of you who prayed over this project.

Thank you to Jesus Christ for loving a sinner like me! My identity is in you now and I look forward to hopefully catching some waves with you one day! With or without the board!

# Rundown of the Chapters

About the Author · · · · · · · · · · · · · · · · · · · · · · · · · · · · v

Foreword · · · · · · · · · · · · · · · · · · · · · · · · · · · · · · · · · · ix

A Few Thank You's · · · · · · · · · · · · · · · · · · · · · · · · · · · · xi

Welcome to your Journey · · · · · · · · · · · · · · · · · · · xvii

Day 1   Being in Awe! · · · · · · · · · · · · · · · · · · · · · · · · · 1

Day 2   Are You Alive? · · · · · · · · · · · · · · · · · · · · · · · · · 5

Day 3   Showtime · · · · · · · · · · · · · · · · · · · · · · · · · · · · 11

Day 4   Who is God? · · · · · · · · · · · · · · · · · · · · · · · · · · 16

Day 5   Who Dat Guy? · · · · · · · · · · · · · · · · · · · · · · · · · 21

Day 6   Count the Cost, Not the Benjamins · · · · · · · · · · 27

Day 7   Please Help! · · · · · · · · · · · · · · · · · · · · · · · · · · 31

Day 8   I Don't Get It · · · · · · · · · · · · · · · · · · · · · · · · · 36

Day 9   What the Boat, Peter? · · · · · · · · · · · · · · · · · · · 40

Day 10  Follow Me · · · · · · · · · · · · · · · · · · · · · · · · · · · 45

Day 11   Hey! Look Here! · · · · · · · · · · · · · · · · · · · · · · · 57
Day 12   Praying · · · · · · · · · · · · · · · · · · · · · · · · · · · 61
Day 13   Skate for Christ · · · · · · · · · · · · · · · · · · · · · · 67
Day 14   Tell em All! · · · · · · · · · · · · · · · · · · · · · · · · 74
Day 15   You Want Pizza! · · · · · · · · · · · · · · · · · · · · · · 78
Day 16   Identity · · · · · · · · · · · · · · · · · · · · · · · · · · · 84
Day 17   Don't Let Your Past Define You · · · · · · · · · · · · · 88
Day 18   Stabbed In The Back · · · · · · · · · · · · · · · · · · · 94
Day 19   Dating/Friends · · · · · · · · · · · · · · · · · · · · · · 101
Day 20   What You Worried About? · · · · · · · · · · · · · · · 107
Day 21   Making Good Choices · · · · · · · · · · · · · · · · · 115
Day 22   I Got You Man! · · · · · · · · · · · · · · · · · · · · · · 121
Day 23   How to Stay in Awe · · · · · · · · · · · · · · · · · · · 127
Day 24   Overcome Your Fear · · · · · · · · · · · · · · · · · · · 132
Day 25   Move! Do Something! Be Radical! · · · · · · · · · · · 140
Day 26   Return · · · · · · · · · · · · · · · · · · · · · · · · · · · 145
Day 27   Never Alone · · · · · · · · · · · · · · · · · · · · · · · · 149
Day 28   Passionately Pursue Your Purpose · · · · · · · · · · · 154
Day 29   You Want me to do What? · · · · · · · · · · · · · · · 159
Day 30   Pick Your Head Up and Get Back in There · · · · · · 166
Day 31   Skyidiving with Jesus · · · · · · · · · · · · · · · · · · 172

Conclusion · · · · · · · · · · · · · · · · · · · · · · · · · · · 179

# Welcome to your Journey

To begin, Chad and I are super pumped that you are taking the time to read this book. Whether it was given to you as a gift or you picked it up off the shelf because the title intrigued you, whatever the reason, I am praying right now that it impacts your life.

We have both spoken at camps and worked with thousands of students and adults over the last ten years. During that time, we have seen God do incredible things, including many "high points" at the end of retreats or mission trips. Moments where you feel like you are ready to go storm the gates of hell and preach at statues. We have also been asked this question time and again: "Now what?" That is the goal of this book, to take you on a journey from fear to faith. We want to see God do incredible things in and through you and to see you live that exhilarating life that only He can provide.

Take this book; read it one day at a time. Read it like we are sitting in the room with you just having a conversation. That is why we wrote it like we did, just us being us. Do not, please hear me, *do not* read ahead. Seek the face of God as you read through each day. Ask Him to speak to you personally. Take time to meditate on the questions we ask, and allow God to move in your heart. If you need to spend more than one day on it, do so. There is no prize for who can get done first; it is not a race. It is a journey.

Be honest with yourself as you go through this. No one is judging you or telling you if your answer is right or wrong. Write in this book, highlight sections, and then go back at times to see how you are growing. This is between you and God. There is no magic ink in the pages that sends your answers to Chad and me (even though that would be legit). If you feel comfortable, go through it with a group of friends so that you can challenge one another and hold one another accountable.

Finally, pray over each day, and allow God's spirit to ultimately be the one who works in and changes you. His working is going to make way more of an impact than anything we will say.

We are praying for you as you take this journey with us.

*Day 1*

---

# Being in Awe!

*When I look at your heavens, the work of your fingers, the moon and the stars, which you have set in place, what is man that you are mindful of him, and the son of man that you care for him?*

PSALM 8:34

*In the hope of eternal life, which God, who cannot lie, promised long ages ago.*

TITUS 1:2

We are super excited that you have chosen to step up and join us on this journey into a thriving relationship with the crazy awesome Jesus. Stop! Before you go any further, check this out...you are alive! I hope you are, or the fact you are reading this is super weird and the zombie apocalypse has started. *Walking Dead* joke, but anyhow, think about that for a moment. Not the zombie thing but about *life*. What if you never existed? This is crazy! Why are you here? How did you get here? These are some of the epic questions we hope to help you find the answers to each day. Right now, the earth is spinning at a little over one thousand miles per hour. How on God's green earth are you not floating around in outer space trying to suck air like a blowfish? It takes the sun's light 8.3 minutes just to reach the earth. Light travels at 186,000 miles per second, which means that my mind is now blown and will need a moment to recover. The universe is huge, and God is bigger. This stuff is ridiculous to even think about. There are between one hundred and two hundred billion galaxies. Check this out: if you were to travel the speed of light across just our galaxy (the Milky Way), it would take you one hundred thousand years to get to the other side. What? OK, I'm freaking out...happy dance!

The universe is insanely large, and the crazy thing is that God says He holds the whole thing in the span of His hand. Isaiah 40:12 says, "Who has measured the waters in the hollow of His hand, and marked off the heavens by the span, and calculated the dust of the earth by the measure, and weighed the mountains in a balance and the hills in a pair of scales?" In this verse the span of a man's hand is from the tip of his pinky finger to the tip of his thumb. So, you know that surfer symbol (the shaka), yeah, that's how God measures the universe. So anytime you are feeling like you need a daily boost, just throw up a shaka symbol with your hand to remind yourself God holds all things from His pinky to His thumb. It's in His hands—not just the world but everything. God is letting you know He's got this!

The God of the universe made all this crazy stuff so that He could give you and me a place to hang out with Him. The stars were hung to bring God glory and so that you could look up and see how amazing He is. You are sitting there, hopefully not on the toilet, reading this book because God wanted you alive! There is literally no chance you get to read this book without God. If God doesn't exist, then there is nothing to bring the something into existence. Fo shizzi!

So you're telling me there's a chance? Sorry, there was my *Dumb and Dumber* movie plug. In *Dumb and Dumber*, Jim Carey totally digs this girl, but she doesn't like him...at all. Jim asks what his chances are of dating her, and she says, "Not good." Then he says, "You mean, not good like one out of a hundred?" She says, "I'd say more like one out of a million." He pauses in concern, which turns to a smile, and says, "So you're telling me there's a chance. Yeah!" OK, I'm weird, but the point is the odds were astronomical, and he was stoked anyway...LOL.

In our story with God, it is a for-sure thing...God wants you! God knew you would struggle, disobey, and do all the other crazy things we get into and still said, "I want you." The star you look at tonight was put there for His glory but also so you could have that moment with Him. The cloud you look at and think is shaped like a kitten or Justin Bieber was put there so you could turn your attention to God. Not the Bieber. You are alive, and now it's time to start figuring out how to live. God loves you and wants you more than the entire universe He created. You were and are worth it. Take a moment to think about what you just read. You can never say again that you are not loved. You are loved so insanely, so ridiculously, we can't even understand it, and that's why it can be tough sometimes. Get ready for this journey 'cause it's gonna be intense. You are gonna laugh, maybe pee in your pants, cry tears of joy, and find peace. Most importantly you are gonna find your true identity. Don't just believe what you see, believe what God said. Be in *awe* today!

What reaction do you have when you read about how big the universe is but that God has the whole world in His hands?

Ask yourself who God says you are, and write it in the space below.

Stop and say a prayer and ask God what He wants to reveal to you through this journey we are going on together. What do you want God to reveal to you?

*Day 2*

# Are You Alive?

*Because of His great love God who is rich in
mercy made us alive with Christ even when
we were dead in transgressions—it is by
grace you have been saved. And God raised
us up with Christ and seated us with him
in the heavenly realms in Christ Jesus.*

EPHESIANS 2:5–6

Have you ever seen *The Walking Dead*? No? LOL...good. I love the show, but it is intense. Basically, people get infected with a disease or something and then start becoming zombies. There is a group of people who try to make a life during the chaos, with zombies trying to eat them. Forgive me, but man, it's in the show. Zombies are nuts! The zombies are the walking dead, and they all follow one another in herds. There really is no purpose for them other than scaring the Buddha out of us. They just follow one another all day long and occasionally run into the living. Sound a little familiar?

Let me explain. So many people are living lives with no purpose! People are dealing with more emotional stress and anxiety than ever before. In our culture we follow the trends like a herd. If a star we love wears certain clothes or looks a certain way, we mimic them. If our friends start dressing a certain way and it becomes popular, we follow suit. We start to live like everyone else around us simply because the people around us are doing it. This becomes a problem when students and others lose their own identity. You might not even know you are doing this until you have lost yourself in the mix of the herd. There could be days you don't want to get out of bed. Almost every day feels too much like the last one. Have you asked yourself "Who am I?" lately?

I fell into this trap when I was a teenager, and it led me down a long path of losing myself. I wanted to be tough when I wasn't, which led me to be mean, and then my heart became hard. Is there a trait in you, or an emotion, that has become a part of you that you wish wasn't there? You might want to be caring and loving and instead you developed fear and bitterness. You might want to be a more passionate person, but something stole your drive. Something or someone hurt you. Now you follow the path of the person in front of you or next to you. Ever stood in line for an amusement park ride for two hours? You literally stood behind the person in front of you in 672-degree heat with sweat in places you didn't know existed. Then got on the ride that lasted 5.2 seconds, stepped off, and wanted to punch yourself in the face for the wasted time you cannot get back. I have.

I remember in high school asking myself if this was all there was to life—following what others are doing for hours out of a day for maybe a few seconds of self-approval. Wake up, go to school, try to fit in, and get decent grades while not disappointing your parents or anyone else. All while also trying to be an athlete and impress your coaches and teammates. I never set a bar or goal to be reached. I just wanted to be good enough for my inner circle of people around me. This is a very lazy approach to life. I don't want to live with regrets, but if I did do it over, I would have realized life isn't about being like or as good as the person next to me. I was put here for a reason and, given my personality and traits, to live out who I am and to pave a path of passion, drive, and adventure. Life would have been so much more fun had I stepped back and found what made me special about being me. I couldn't feel special or know who I was when I was constantly flooded with thoughts about everyone else. People can tell you that you are special all day long, but if you don't believe it, then those true words register as false in your mind. You are special because you are God's creation. You become what you see, think, hear, and say. Look at how you are living. What are you watching? What are you thinking? What or who are you listening to? What are you saying to yourself and others? You will become whatever that is. Adjust these things now, and see amazing changes take place.

Sometimes if you change your environment, you can change your life.

Check it! One of my favorite songs right now is by We Are Messengers; it is called "Magnify." It says:

> *But just a glimpse draws*
> *my heart to change*
> *And one side of you lays*
> *my sin to waste*

The writer realizes that without knowing this life-giving Spirit, he might not be able to hold on. He also understands that he won't know everything, but just the glimpse, the something that he does focus on, is more than enough to give him life and a change of heart. Have you caught a glimpse of God lately, or are your heart and eyes on other people so much that you can't even catch a glimpse? All you need is one moment with this God, and He can change *everything*. The chorus says:

> *Take it all take it all away*
> *Magnify no other name*
> *Open up open up my eyes*
> *To you*

Ask God to open up your eyes today. Maybe there is something you are missing. Maybe a slight pause during the day would help you catch a glimpse of Him. Take a pause, and don't lift up everything else in your life…completely lift up Jesus. Jesus, You rock!

You are amazing. I might not even feel You right now, but I place myself in Your presence. I want You to make me alive right now. I'm Yours! His prayer in the song is this:

> *God be greater than*
> *the worries in my life,*
> *Be stronger than the*
> *weakness in my mind,*

Wow! The power here comes from lifting up God and not himself. God, be bigger than my emotions…be bigger than my laziness…be bigger than my doubt! Do this today. Ask God to be bigger than everything that's holding you back from an insanely cool relationship with Him. Don't focus on the test; go use your testimony.

> *When life knocks you down, try to land on your back. Because if you can look up, you can get up. Let your reason get you back up*
> —Motivational speaker Les Brown

Have you ever felt like every day is the same and wonder if there is more? How can you start living?

Write down all the things you want God to be bigger than in your life. It might be struggles, relationships, or anything else that comes to mind.

How can you apply the words in this chapter to your life? Really think through it.

*Day 3*

# Showtime

*You are a mist that appears for a
little while and then vanishes.*

*JAMES 4:14*

This is one of those verses I have read over many times in life, but it was not until the last few years that it has really hit me just how true it is. Our lives are but a vapor that could be here today and gone tomorrow. Working with kids has really made me think about that fact and hopefully will make you think about it too. Notice I said *fact*—your life will end; it is one of the few guarantees we have in this life.

Let me paint an image in your mind to start this day off. Here we are, a group of twelve of us in Washington, DC, skating

Freedom Plaza. It's about ninety-five degrees outside, bright-blue sky, and let me just say, it is a perfect day. It is a completely care-free time, just taking in those moments that you remember in life. Around one o'clock we all decided to gather up for a break for lunch when we hear some commotion off in the distance. Like most people, it caught our attention. What we noticed, though, was heartbreaking. Three businessmen dressed in their finest were making fun of an obviously homeless man, mocking him, spitting on him, and just causing problems. He was wearing a North Carolina starter winter jacket in the middle of this heat and carrying around three massive garbage bags as well as a paper bag hiding his alcohol. Let me say this, though: I was proud of the way the skaters handled it, not joining in but showing concern for this guy.

Next thing we know, he notices us and starts making his way toward us. Stumbling a little bit, he begins to put his hand up to his mouth with his pointer finger and pinky raised and starts to whisper, "It's Showtime." At first, we are taken aback a little bit because he just keeps whispering this statement. "It's Showtime!" He doesn't come over asking for money or a handout but just wants someone to talk to. So here we are, and we just begin listening to his story. He starts out by asking us if we had ever been to Arizona. "No," we all reply, and he says, "Good, cuz I rob banks there." With that statement we all just keep listening, wondering what he is talking about. Then he begins to say "showtime" again. Only this time he is telling us that Showtime is his nickname and that he got that name from friends who knew him in Arizona. The story continued on for probably fifteen minutes more, with the idea that when it came to robbing banks, he had eight minutes to get in and get out before the police would show up. For him, that eight minutes, that was his showtime. If he didn't finish, he would be busted, so he had to make the most of that time. He shared the idea that he had a mental clock telling just how much time he had. Whether his stories were true or not, I may never know. Either way, I will never forget that day or that encounter, and I am sure the guys who were with me would probably say the same thing.

After Showtime left us that day, we all sat back, trying to take in what we had just experienced, but what came out of it I would have never imagined. We talked about the idea of what we would change if we all knew exactly how much time we had left to live. Like a clock in front of us counting down our minutes. Showtime knew he had eight minutes.

Really think about this. What if I told you that you had one year left. Dave, you have eight years. Tom, you have seventy-two years. Mike, you have three days. If we could literally keep tabs on how much time we had left, would we change how we live, the conversations we have, the choices we'd make? If you are like me, I can almost guarantee each and every one of us would say yes to that question. Here is the thing, though: we do not have that clock in front of us, so we must learn to make the most of every moment before our clock runs out. Are there things you would change? I am a big country fan, and the song "Live Like You Were Dying" by Tim McGraw talks about this idea: "Skydiving, Rocky Mountain climbing, I went 2.7 seconds on a bull named Fu Manchu." Then a movie came out called *The Bucket List*, and it was all about the things the characters wanted to do before they kicked the bucket. So many times we just look at that idea and go "Nah, not me, I have a ton of life left to live." But what if you don't? It is not a guarantee but a vapor.

I am not writing this day to give you a reason to go buck wild, like the new motto YOLO (You Only Live Once). I am writing this chapter to tell you that you never know how much time you have. As Christians we should live in a way that we desire to bring God glory through every day of our lives. Making *our* lives His showtime. What is He calling you to do? Are you going to follow after Him, seeking Him daily, saying, "God, what do You have for me now?" My worry is that when we stand before Him one day, many will make the statement, "God, I just thought I had more time!" As we start diving into this book together, I want you to really think about whether you are living your showtime. Chad and I want to challenge you to make the most of every moment.

If you knew how much time you had to live, what would you do differently?

What would be on your bucket list?

Will you start making your showtime today? Be specific with how, and really challenge yourself.

## Day 4

## Who is God?

*For I am the Lord your God who takes*
*hold of your right hand and says to you,*
*Do not fear; I will help you.*

ISAIAH 41:13

Earlier today my two-year-old pooped in her diaper and then tried to change it herself. Long story short, it did not go so well. A valiant effort, but let's just say we must wash everything. Elmo does not look the same...LOL. My bad, I know that's gross, but such is life, to be honest. The gross, crazy things can be some of the best, most memorable moments.

I'll never forget when I was eighteen and on a college holiday when I went to a party with a group of friends. The girl I had a crush on since I was in the womb was gonna be there, and at the time, I thought she had never seen me as more than my cousin's cousin. (Yeah, you can e-mail me for my family tree.) So we drive to this hotel and hang out for a while. Another buddy and I hadn't had much to drink, but another friend of ours had maybe a little more than he should have to be driving. We let him drive (bad move) and set off on the forty-five-minute drive home. As we got closer to home, we were doing about seventy in a forty-five, and a cop turned around and did the "whoop, whoop" thing. (That's my best siren noise.) Well, it turns out my friend had a suspended license, and he tried to lose the cop by pulling off into a neighborhood. He turned off the lights and parked, but the police officer was on us. My buddy asked one of us to switch seats with him so that he wouldn't get in trouble, and of course, yours truly was like "Dude, I got you." Within thirty seconds I had maybe six police officers with guns pointed at me because they thought I was driving. I went to jail for a night, but the whole thing got worked out because my friend ended up telling them the whole truth.

All that being said, my parents were upset. Before this happened, they had been wanting me to attend a school that could get me focused. I didn't know God had laid a certain school on their hearts. I was going to a division-three school at the time as a walk-on football and basketball player. I don't even remember going to class. My grades were terrible because I didn't care at all. My parents were like "Listen, you are going to Liberty University." I said, "The Christian school?" LOL.

If I had not gone through that crazy night, I might not have ever gone to Liberty, where my life changed drastically. For starters,

I met Josh, the crazy guy who sounds stoned. He is the other author of this book…and he doesn't smoke weed. He just sounds like it. Cracks me up. Anyway, so I met God at Liberty as well. Like the real God. Not the one we go to church for and pretend to know or the one someone preaches at us and then we never do anything about it or figure out for ourselves what we believe. The real freakin' deal. (Yes, I said freakin'.) So before you go any further, let me help you understand this God a little bit. This way, when you get into the Bible, it makes sense, and you don't have to make stuff up. A major goal is to know the Bible well enough to where you can separate what is your mind and what God is actually saying.

God is eternal. He is independent of time and space. He exists whether people want Him to or not, and time is relative to Him. Time does not hold our God to specific moments. He was and is and always will be. He cannot die, and He was not created. (We will talk about Jesus in days coming up, so chillax on that one for a bit).

He is immutable. He cannot change and will never change. He cannot become less or worse. He cannot become more or greater. He is perfect and therefore cannot become more perfect because perfection is perfect. Ha! Mind explosion. If He could become less or more, He would not be perfect and therefore could not be God.

He is omniscient. He knows all things: in our minds, in the physical realm, in our relationships, and so on. He does not even have to think about it; He just knows it. Every thought and everything, He grasps at all times and in all scenarios. That's pretty cool!

The one thing I really want you to take away is that God cannot lie, and if that is so, then when He tells you He loves you, or you have a purpose, it is a fact. There is nothing you can do about it. He loves you. *You* are here for a reason. God had the ability to create anyone, and He decided He wanted Billy Bieber, Mariah Carey Jr., or whatever your name is. God knows your thoughts. He knows everything about you, and you can't escape His love for you, no matter how hard you try. So think about the idea for today…God cannot lie! As you read further and we dive into this crazy adventure, remember when you read something from God, it is a fact. If He says you are loved insanely…that's a fact. We want you to get to the point where you can't imagine spending a moment without God. Where you are so passionate and in love with Him that you can't wait to hear Him speak to you again. If He says, "Jump," then you say, "How high?" Get to know God. Just going to church and thinking everything is gonna change is like parking a car in a garage and thinking the car will turn into a garage. It ain't hap'nin'. Go after Him. He is already coming to you.

Google, or otherwise look up somehow, all the things the Bible says about God. God is…what?

Who is God to you?

Is your view of God based on people, the world, or Scripture? Why?

*Day 5*

# Who Dat Guy?

*When Jesus came to the region of Caesarea
Philippi, he asked his disciples, "Who do people
say the Son of Man is?" They replied, "Some
say John the Baptist; others say Elijah; and
still others, Jeremiah or one of the prophets."*

*MATTHEW 16:13–14*

A question I believe we all need to ask ourselves is: Who is Jesus to me? When talking about Jesus, do you talk about Him in personal terms? Or do you just know Him through what others have said about Him? Let's look at today's passage to understand what I mean. This has truly turned into one of my favorite passages to read, to teach, and to hear how others respond. Jesus starts out by asking the simple question, "Who do others say that I am?" It is kind of a peculiar question if you think about it. Is Jesus really worried about what others are saying about Him? Maybe, or possibly it is just His way of getting His disciples prepared for the next question He will ask, which we will get to in a little bit.

Some say John the Baptist, which in itself is a strange answer, considering John the Baptist was alive at the same time as Jesus. Others say He is an Old Testament prophet and so forth. In today's culture it seems that everyone has an opinion of who Jesus is. Oprah says this, Madonna says that, a Baptist says this, and a Catholic says that. Everyone seems to have their own thoughts. A. W. Tozer says this in *The Pursuit of God*:

> *To most people God is an inference, not a reality. He is a deduction from evidence, but he remains personally unknown to the individual. Others do not even go as far as this, they know of him only from hearsay. They have not bothered to think the matter out for themselves, but have heard about it from others.[1]*

All I can come up with, though, in today's age, is what He is truly saying is: "Do you know me by what others say about me?" Like do you know Jesus as what others have said, like your youth pastor or your parents or what some celebrity says about Him? Is that how you respond when asked about Jesus? Do you give answers that are based on a song lyric that maybe you have sung time and again?

---

1  A. W. Tozer, *The Pursuit of God* (Bloomington, MN: Bethany House, 2013), 22.

I have asked this question a lot, and I get some off-the-wall answers. Well, my parents say this, or my pastor says that. "He's my shepherd." I remember getting that one from an inner-city kid who had never been near a farm in his life. I just looked at him and had to ask, "Do you even know what a shepherd does?" He replied honestly, "No, but I thought it sounded good." Or the classic answer: "Well, I read this somewhere online."

Think about it. How would you describe Jesus? Who do others in your life say Jesus is?

*"But what about you?" he asked. "Who do you say I am?" Simon Peter answered, "You are the Messiah, the Son of the living God"* (Matthew 16:15–16).

Now to the heart of it and why I love this passage so much. In this passage Jesus declares He wants a personal relationship with you. Picture this with me, Him walking squarely up to you, looking you in the eyes, mano a mano, and asking, "Who am I to you?" Then, again, He asks a little more emphatically. WHO? Pause. AM? Pause. I? Pause. TO? Pause. YOU? Period.

You start with your answer of a song lyric or a sermon you heard your pastor say, and Jesus cuts you off. "We are now on to the personal side of this. I didn't ask who others say I am anymore; I asked who am I to you?" Hmmm, kind of dumbfounded, not really sure how to answer, waiting to see if someone else will speak up, then out of nowhere you hear a voice. Peter, being who he is, blunt and bold, steps up. "You are the Messiah. Son of the living God." Bam! Peter got it. Jesus was personal. How did Peter come up with that? Let's continue on in this passage:

*Jesus replied, "Blessed are you, Simon son of Jonah, for this was not revealed to you by flesh and blood, but by my Father in heaven"* (Matthew 16:17).

God revealed it to him. That's how! I believe that He wants to reveal to each and every one of us who Jesus is personally through different experiences we have in life. Did you hear me with that? God Himself wants to reveal to you the truth about who Jesus is in your life. It isn't meant to be a mystery or something you struggle with; He wants you to know!

Let me present it this way. If I asked you to describe to me who my wife is to you, you would have no clue because you have never met her. Or if you asked me to describe you, I most likely wouldn't have an answer because I have never encountered you. But if you asked me to describe my wife, I could go on and on about who she is because I have a personal relationship with her, and things about her have been revealed to me. Or if I asked your parents the question, "Tell me about your kid," I am sure they could tell me all sorts of things, good and bad. In life we learn about others because of spending time with them.

Now think about it again in terms of Jesus asking the question. How has Jesus revealed Himself to you? How has He been revealed in your life? I want to finish this chapter with two of the most personal answers I have ever heard.

First was a girl about twenty-two years old who stood up with tears in her eyes and said, "Jesus is my knight in shining armor."

(I thought, "Oh great, another sappy answer.") She continued to share how she had just gotten engaged, and within a week after that, her fiancé was deployed. Fighting back the tears, she said she got the call that her love had been killed in action. It was in that moment she truly had to lean on her faith to heal her heart. Talk about a personal answer!

The second was one of our skaters; he started out by saying this might not be the correct or church answer, but it was the best he had. "Jesus to me is like the first dip of Copenhagen I get in the morning." (He had my attention!) "He is my addiction that I need every morning. The days I don't spend with Him in the morning affect my whole day. I will get headaches, I will be grumpy, and just annoyed by everyone. But when I get my Jesus, it is like getting my dip. It is getting my dose of happy." I wish I could make this up. But it was personal. So now I ask you, take the time to think about it.

Who have others told you Jesus is?

Now who is Jesus to you?

Do you realize that as you continue to go through life, God will continue to reveal Jesus more personally to you?

Tell me why that thought excites you?

*Day 6*

# Count the Cost, Not the Benjamins

*And whoever does not carry their cross and
follow me cannot be my disciple. Suppose one
of you wants to build a tower. Won't you first
sit down and estimate the cost to see if you have
enough money to complete it? For if you lay the
foundation and are not able to finish it, everyone
who sees it will ridicule you, saying, "This person
began to build and wasn't able to finish."*

*Luke 14:27–30*

Welcome to day six. You will need some deodorant, a toothbrush, and golf ball. OK, in all seriousness, you might need some deodorant because the topic could make you sweat. I didn't wear deodorant the other day, and I had a meeting at Starbucks. I was wearing a tank top, and when I lifted my arms above my head, I gagged. Yep, I was like what just... oh, it's me. So...smell good, and you can lift your hands above your head.

Listen, a while ago I had my whole family at the grocery store, and we were buying a lot of food and things to stock up so we didn't have to keep going back. Kalyssa, my two-year-old, was screaming in the aisles, so we had to find ways to make her happy. Usually this means one of us getting an Elmo doll or running her through aisles so she thinks she is flying. Lexi, our seven-year-old, loves attention, so she is dancing and singing Taylor Swift songs and trying to make everyone watch her. So then I join in and become even more loud and obnoxious. She hates it; I love it. As we go to the checkout line with a cart full of items, Kalyssa gets a few more screams out, and I pretend that I don't know whose child she is. "Whose kid is that? Get control; we all just want some peace...man!" My wife gives me an irritated look, and it makes me laugh more. Why? I don't know. The checkout person scans all our items, and we go to pay but it says insufficient funds. Now I'm embarrassed, and I run. I didn't, but I wanted to. There are like 622 people behind us because it's Walmart, and why not have only three registers open? I love Walmart...just kidding. It turns out we got paid the day before, and we had just paid bills and bought new stuff for the family, so we didn't thoroughly go through our finances before we got there.

Check this out…Jesus asks us to count the cost before we decide to take this journey with Him:

*And whoever does not carry their cross and follow me cannot be my disciple. Suppose one of you wants to build a tower. Won't you first sit down and estimate the cost to see if you have enough money to complete it? For if you lay the foundation and are not able to finish it, everyone who sees it will ridicule you, saying, "This person began to build and wasn't able to finish"* (Luke 14:27–30).

The truth is that most people do not count the cost before they decide to follow Jesus. The American church talks a lot about *what* they can get instead of *who* they are getting. Jesus is letting us know that following Him is going to cost you everything. We must first be willing to give everything away emotionally and mentally before saying we are followers physically. You have life only because Christ gave it to you, so in order to live an abundant life, you must emotionally be willing to abandon everything for the person of Jesus Christ. You might be ridiculed or bullied or even lose your life. When other people are doing the wrong thing, will you stand up and do what God wants you to do? I didn't count the cost before I went shopping that day, and in turn, we didn't get the groceries and felt embarrassed. Have you counted the cost today as you get into the rest of this book? Jesus gave it all for you; are you willing to give it all for Him? If you want eternal love, you have to be willing to lose temporary pleasures.

What does the phrase "count the cost" mean to you?

Do you worry a lot about what other people may think of you? Do you ever stop to think about what God thinks of you? Why or why not?

What do you think it means to be "all in" for Jesus?

## Day 7

# Please Help!

*For the word of God is alive and active. Sharper*
*than any double-edged sword, it penetrates even*
*to dividing soul and spirit, joints and marrow; it*
*judges the thoughts and attitudes of the heart.*

*HEBREWS 4:12*

So here you are, leaving camp or church or wherever, totally on fire for Christ but being sent out into the world feeling like you are all alone. The only advice your youth pastor gives you is to get into the Word. You get home, you look at what seems like a massive book (anything over one hundred pages I consider massive), and you really want to do this. You have all the ambition and desire in the world, but then…you honestly have no clue where to start. All the book names are crazy, with tons of letters that you can't pronounce. You ask yourself, "Do I start in the Old or New Testament, whatever that means?," and you are honestly just confused. You aren't alone. I remember when I first got to Liberty University (so you know I didn't get saved until my senior year of high school) and other students were throwing out these big words of theology. Talking about all the stuff they had memorized and getting into debates, and I just looked and said, "I got Jesus. I love Jesus, and I want to share Him." I had no clue beyond that. I was in the same boat as you, completely confused when it came to Scripture.

I have to make a confession. Even though I am in ministry and have been for years, I am still horrible at understanding Scripture and really diving in to get to know its meaning. It confuses me, it frustrates me, and at times I want to give up. Sound like you? If so, let me try to help you.

First off, take a moment and ask the Spirit to guide you through and enlighten you when it comes to your reading. The book of James says that if you need wisdom, ask for it. Reading Scripture itself is a perfect example of that. God wants you to understand it; He didn't give us the Word to confuse and frustrate us but for us to enjoy and know Him. So please, if you don't hear anything else I say on this day, learn to stop and say, "God, I want to know your Word; please help me to understand."

A second key factor that I have found to be helpful is to have a pen or highlighter and a notebook on hand. Others may not agree with me on this, but as you read and understand something, make notes in your Bible so that when you start reading again, you can look back and see how your thoughts change as you grow. My own personal Bible is beat up and filled with notes, some years and years old. It is always awesome, though, to look back and see how much I have changed.

Some of the best advice I ever got about reading the Bible and actually understanding it was to put myself into the stories. To truly embrace the scene, to close my eyes and daydream of being there and picking out pieces of the story that I could understand and relate to. For example, if the passage is talking about Jesus going to a mountainside, envision the last time you went snowboarding and the scenery around you. Or if it talks about Him being at the lake, picture the last time you went camping. You get my gist? Hope that helps.

Maybe the issue for you is that you are just stuck on where to start. For some they will recommend just praying and then opening your Bible and where you turn to is where God wants you. (I am not a fan of that strategy because I like to get the full picture of sections I am reading and not being all over the place each day, but like I said, this does work for others.) I always like to recommend starting with the Gospels in order to get a picture of who Jesus is. When you start, though, don't skip over the introduction to these books if your Bible has them because it can contain useful information. Another great spot to start is the Psalms, for you truly get to see the human, emotional, vulnerable, and realistic side of King David, and it helps you to realize that others go through the same things you do. This is honestly a choice that is up to you, though, because God can speak through any part of Scripture and teach you something maybe you haven't seen before. No spot is a dumb spot; I am just excited that you are interested and want to read.

Finally, find a mentor to help you understand as you read and to answer your questions. This is where your notebook comes into play. Write down what you don't understand, and know that there are no stupid questions. Ask! There may be times where your mentor will say, "I am not sure, but let's find out together." The truth is I would, and they would, rather you ask the question than never ask at all.

Scripture truly can be life-changing and something you come to love. Don't give up. Keep pressing, knowing God himself gave you the Bible as His continual love story, and He wants you to understand.

> *If anyone lacks wisdom, you should ask God, who gives generously to all without finding fault, and it will be given to you* (James 1:5).

In your own words, what does this verse mean to you when it comes to studying Scripture?

Do you find yourself getting frustrated easily?

Who can you get to help you? I want you to think about this and to write down his or her name now as accountability. When will you ask this person?

## Day 8

---

# I Don't Get It

*Man shall not live by bread alone, but on every
word that comes from the mouth of God.*

*-MATTHEW 4:4*

*"God, what do you want for my life?"*
*"Man, I wish I knew my purpose!"*
*"I really wish I had a manual for life."*

Have you ever uttered one of these statements? If we are being
honest in this book, which is ultimately the goal, I believe
we all have. Everyone, going back to the beginning of time, at
some point or another in their lives, searches for their purpose.
They may even go through moments in life where they feel they

are just wandering aimlessly. Maybe that is you now. I still have my days of feeling that way, where I will wake up and go, "God, You know this life would be so much easier if You just gave me a ten-step program to follow and check off." If that is you, perfect; let's read on together:

> *Thy word is a lamp unto my feet and a light unto my path* (Psalm 119:105).

In this passage, David gives us the answer to all those earlier questions. He tells us that the answers to life's greatest questions are found right here within this book, the Bible. We have the answers right there collecting dust on our shelves as we continue to question God about what He wants, and it is like He is in the room, screaming, "I *want* to show you; open the book up!" But you are looking at it, and the excuses start flowing in your mind:

> "That dusty old thing written two thousand years ago, how can it help me?"
> "Well, I don't understand it."
> "It's old-fashioned."
> "I don't like to read."
> "I don't have time."

Think about this with me in correlation with doing homework or preparing for a test. You have an assignment to do and reading is involved. Can you imagine going to your teacher and saying, "Well, I thought that book was old-fashioned, so I didn't read it." Better yet, imagine this one with me, "Well, you see, Doc, I didn't understand, so I just quit on it." Or probably the most famous excuse of all, "I just didn't have time." All of which I can only imagine him looking at you and laughing, as he hands you the test and says good luck.

Now follow me here—your life is that test. God wants us to know how to live, to know what His purpose is for us, and to find joy in it. It isn't His fault if we choose not to pick up the manual. Here we are, continuing to wander through life, falling off the cliff, and God is begging us to just pick up the map. I have to say this, though: I do understand that Scripture can be confusing. If that is you, do like you would in a class: seek help, get a mentor, and allow someone to coach you on the ways of God.

OK, one final thought on this for you: think of the Bible like food. Your stomach is growling like crazy, over and over. You are at the point where you are getting physically ill because you haven't eaten. You know the answer, the food is right there in front of you, saying, "Eat me." Yet for some reason you just keep looking at it. Instead of opening the pizza box, "yummm, pizza," and taking care of your craving, you come up with an excuse, something like "But then I'd have to open the box." So instead you just let it sit there. Now, it might sound ridiculous, but Scripture is food for our souls. It is the Bread of Life. We will go to every extreme to make sure we are fed physically, yet when it comes to feeding our spirit, we starve it. Then we wonder why we feel exhausted, drained, frustrated, and lost at times. Maybe, just maybe—did I say maybe?—that is God's way of telling you to eat. You are meant to eat! Now feed that starving spirit already.

What questions do you have about God's plans for you?

Do you believe that God wants you to know the answers?

What are your excuses for not seeking those answers in the Bible?

## Day 9

## What the Boat, Peter?

*"Come," he said. Then Peter got down out of the*
*boat, walked on the water and came toward Jesus.*

-*MATTHEW 14:29*

What's up wit yah self, home skillet? I am literally praying as I write this that you are at a point where you are making some serious strides into what it means to know Jesus. The further you go into this journal, the more risks you take. We are going to challenge you to see this world through an entirely different lens. We want you to skydive with Jesus. That means we want you to understand that your maximum joy is right on the other side of your maximum fear. You might be afraid to follow

Jesus because of what others will think of you. Maybe you watch porn and do drugs, so you don't think He will keep forgiving you. You might be so afraid of failure that you never try anything you are passionate about. You have failed before, and someone told you how horrible you were or how you will never make it. Maybe your whole plan is actually your parents' plan for your life, and then my question is: "Are you sure your parents know the plan God has for you?" Are you afraid you won't fit in? Do you have a bully? Are you addicted and feel terrible inside? Have you been abused and don't think anyone could ever love you again? Have you become angry and bitter, and it has made you become a mean person? Are you trying to be someone you are not? Has fear made your heart hard? In this life, if you don't recognize it, you won't realize it.

There is an insane story in the Bible, and it freaks me out at times. Here is the story of Jesus walking on water:

*Immediately Jesus made the disciples get into the boat and go on ahead of him to the other side, while he dismissed the crowd. After he had dismissed them, he went up on a mountainside by himself to pray. Later that night, he was there alone, and the boat was already a considerable distance from land, buffeted by the waves because the wind was against it. Shortly before dawn Jesus went out to them, walking on the lake. When the disciples saw him walking on the lake, they were terrified. "It's a ghost," they said, and cried out in fear. But Jesus immediately said to them: "Take courage! It is I.*

*Don't be afraid." "Lord, if it's you," Peter replied, "tell me to come to you on the water." "Come," he said. Then Peter got down out of the boat, walked on the water and came toward Jesus. But when he saw the wind, he was afraid and, beginning to sink, cried out, "Lord, save me!" Immediately Jesus reached out his hand and caught him. "You of little faith," he said, "why did you doubt?" And when they climbed into the boat, the wind died down. Then those who were in the boat worshiped him, saying, "Truly you are the Son of God"* (Matthew 14:22–33).

Listen, peeps, I am a surfer, and if I see a dude walking out to me on top of the water, I am losing my mind, or I would be thinking, "What was in that Pepsi?" First, let's acknowledge how ridiculously cool it is that Jesus walked on water. Jesus is the best surfer of all time; move over Kelly Slater. Peter boldly asks Jesus to let him come out and walk on the water with Him. This is super cool! When was the last time you asked God for something bold like that? Not that you would get the newest game system or shoes, but "God, let me be a part of what you are doing. Use me in a mighty way!"

Peter is super stoked, so he probably grabs the edge of the boat, whips his legs over, and is stunned when he realizes he isn't sinking. Then he sees Jesus and starts walking to the God of the universe. Suddenly he hears some thunder, or a wave hits him, and he gets distracted. Fear kicks in. His mind begins to doubt that he will be OK. He starts to sink and then looks up at Jesus, who pulls him out of the situation that started because of his distraction. Peter doubted that God would keep him safe. This is interesting because we are talking about the God of the universe here. He created Peter and wanted him to exist to share the love of Jesus. No matter what happens, Peter is going to get to hang out with Jesus forever, so why not just let God do His thing? Why not just be in the moment with God and be all there? Why can't we be all there with God in the moment?

The moment we take our eyes off of Jesus and begin to rely on ourselves, we are already sinking. We might not even realize we are sinking into a bad situation until something really tangible happens. Part of being a disciple is looking at our lives and seeing what we are distracted by the most so that we can counter it with trust. If I know what I am afraid of, and if I know what distracts me, then I can continue to keep my spiritual eyes on Jesus through the storm. Be active in your walk with God. In order to skydive with Jesus, we need to face our fears and understand why we are afraid. We can start with walking on water today, so ask yourself what distracts you the most. What makes you take your eyes off of Jesus?

When was the last time you took a bold step out onto the water for God?

What distracts you the most from your relationship with God?

What is the biggest fear that is holding you back from skydiving with Jesus?

## Day 10

## Follow Me

*As Jesus was walking beside the Sea of Galilee,*
*he saw two brothers, Simon called Peter and*
*his brother Andrew. They were casting a*
*net into the lake, for they were fishermen.*
*"Come, follow me," Jesus said, "and I will*
*send you out to fish for people." At once*
*they left their nets and followed him.*

MATTHEW *4:18–20*

A few days ago I talked to you about how to read Scripture, and one of the examples I gave you was to put yourself into the story. Let's do that now. Picture yourself as one of the fishermen on the beach with me. What are you thinking and sensing? Is the weather nice? How big are the waves? Truly put yourself into the story. Close your eyes and envision it.

Here you are hanging out at the beach doing some fishing, hoping to catch some dinner. Time is just passing by as you are out there relaxing, just doing your thing, maybe having a little time to clear your head. Maybe you are feeling the pressure that you haven't caught anything yet and that this is your livelihood. Out of nowhere you hear these words: "Hey, you. Come, follow me." You look around and here comes this shabby, bearded, homeless-looking dude walking up to you. At first glance you think, "Oh, that's just Chad, no big deal." Then you hear it once again: "Come, follow me."

Now, in my mind the questions would start flowing: "Where are we going? When are we coming back? Do I need to take anything?" And if you are like me, you start thinking food: "Is the food good where we are going? Is it to the islands? I've always wanted to go back there."

Your mind starts racing. Again, if you are anything like me, it wouldn't take much convincing at all, but I am up always up for a little adventure in my life. Maybe he has you convinced that you should go, but can you imagine making that call home to your parents? "Hey, Mom, I wanted to let you know that this guy Jesus told me to follow Him, and I think I am going to do it." Screaming on the other end of the line starts to ensue:

"Are you going to be safe?"
"Well, He told me I am actually probably going to die."
"Are you able to call and check in each night?"

"Yeah, probably not happening, Mom."
"Can you at least tell me where you are going?"
"Yeah, I don't know that either."

Think about this seriously, the craziness of this story. In today's modern world, we would probably be getting out the fifty-page legal documents about safety, wanting to give Jesus all the fine print of what we think we should be allowed to do and where we can go. Asking all kinds of questions. Maybe we'd say, "Give me a few days to think about this," or pray over it, if you are the type to give spiritual answers. Maybe you are the type who really wants to follow, but you are thinking you have a better way, so you speak up: "I know Your Word says this, Jesus, and You asked me to follow, but I really think we should try it my way." This is where I believe Jesus's humor would come out a little bit: "You're right, Josh, because you got, what, thirty-four years' experience in this thing we call life, and I have what...eternity? Yeah, maybe you're right; we should change all eternity, and let's start following on Josh's terms." Then you realize in His sarcasm His eternal perspective kind of trumps your years of wisdom. OK, Jesus, maybe You're right.

Here, though, it says the disciples up and left their nets at once and went. No questions asked. Did you catch that part? The passage just says "at once." What about you? When you know without a doubt Jesus is calling you to something, to follow Him, do you question, or do you just follow? Now I do a lot of spur-of-the-moment things in my life, lots of crazy stuff, but this seems nuts!

Maybe it is your experience at a youth camp, where the speaker has just finished and asks you in that moment if you want to follow Jesus. You sense in your heart that you were meant for this moment. Yet instead of just following and listening, you look around to see who is sitting beside you. You start worrying about what others will think. You worry what your parents might say or how your leader might respond.

Maybe for you it is a call to missions. God has laid on your heart a certain country or certain area to go to. Maybe it is even your school. Jesus is saying, "Follow me, and I will make you fishers of men." What do you do? Follow or question? Follow or set the terms for Jesus? "I will follow You as long as You keep me safe; I will follow You as long as it doesn't affect my relationship; I will follow You as long as I can have Wi-Fi access—I got to check my Facebook each day. I will follow You as long as..."

Think about this story. How would you have responded?

What is holding you back from following Him?

What are the "as long as" terms you are setting on Jesus leading you?

## Fear to Faith Personal Testimony 1
## Josh Marburger Crazy transitions of Marriage, Multiplying, and Ministry

Skaters love transitions. Watching the Vans Park Series recently with our oldest son, Caleb, we were stoked seeing young men and women boost huge airs and throw creative combinations of grinds and inverts on the fresh "concrete waves" that made up the unique transitions of a new skatepark in Shanghai, China.

If you have ever stood on top of a huge ramp or paddled in to a huge wave and chose to "drop in," you know that transitions can sometimes be fun and sometimes be painful. Dropping in requires focus, but any wise skater—yes that's a thing— will tell you that overthinking something will throw you off your flow and probably throw you off your board as well.

A huge part of the art of skating or surfing is not letting fear trip you up. In the 1991 cult-classic movie, Point Break, the character played by Patrick Swayze famously quips: "Fear causes hesitation, and hesitation will cause your worst fears to come true." Though the movie is full of characters that make selfish choices that lead to death, Patrick Swayze's character is definitely on to something. Hesitation can hurt all of us.

Josh Knipple, a good friend who is a pastor and author, asked me (Joshua) to write about God turning my fear into faith. Both me and Nicole are a work in progress, and fear has paralyzed us many times. Nevertheless, nothing has strengthened our faith more than the scary transitions of marriage, multiplying, and ministry.

May 3, 2008, my beautiful bride, Nicole Haunani Bisera, became Nicole Haunani Marburger after walking down the aisle to meet me at Putnam Baptist Church in Shelby, NC. We had no idea that day when we said, "I do" that for two to live as one meant both of us would die (hopefully not from murder).

The best marriages result from daily dying to self and living as one in Christ. Marriage means we "leave, cleave, and weave." For Nic and I, marriage has meant leaving both our moms and dads (we moved 4500 miles 3 weeks after tying the knot), clinging to each other (which often means letting go of security blankets likes cell phone screens and our individual schedules), and becoming one--- choosing to share all the intimacy of the same bedroom, bank account, and even the same (sometimes stinky) bathroom!

Nicole still calls marriage "the greatest sanctifying agent in her life," because of the struggle for two to be one. Yet, even on the days when we are holding on for dear life; we are reminded of God's "never-stopping, never-giving-up, unbreaking, always-and-forever love" (Sally Lloyd-Jones, The Jesus Storybook Bible). The Most High's love for each of us is the grace that causes us to be gracious and the love that makes us loving toward each other. This is our 10 th year, and though at times this crazy transition of marriage is still rough---as we daily choose faith over fear, we are able to enjoy the ride as one.

The second huge way we have had to learn faith over fear is having babies together (multiplying). Learning to see the world through the eyes of our three boys has grown us to see how dependent we truly are on God and others. Author Tim Keller, in his book Counterfeit God's, wrote: "We are the product of three things—genetics, environment, and our personal choices—but two of these three factors we have no power over." Our oldest two boys love creating with LEGOS, but their buildings and cities are limited by what pieces they have. Knowing that Jesus is the "Master Builder" of our lives, we are comforted that the world is almost like a huge LEGO city made by the Most High God, who is unlimited in what He can make and create as He lovingly writes and builds the story of each of our lives (Hebrews 3:4; 12:1-2). Our kids did nothing to bring themselves into the situations in which they live every day; and yet, like us, they daily choose whether to respond with faith to their parents who love them and have their best interests in mind; or with fear and disobedience thinking their own ways are better (even at their ages of 5, 3, and 1 year old).

This transition of having babies has shown us that we need to be like babies in the loving arms of our heavenly father. We try to focus on the truth that Jesus highly valued children saying "Let the little children come to me, and do not hinder them, for the kingdom of heaven belongs to such as these" (Matthew 19:14). Also, we work to remember that Jesus said: "Truly I tell you, unless you change and become like little children, you will never enter the kingdom of heaven" (Matthew 18:3). Nicole and I are still learning how to obey God as His son and daughter while helping our boys see God's loving hand on their lives. We know that thousands of years ago the fear of God's people, followed by pessimism and inaction, led almost a whole generation to miss out on the Promised Land. Though the transition of having babies has given us new schedules (what's sleep?), new financial responsibilities (how many times can you reuse a diaper?), and different entertainment (who knew cardboard boxes could be so fun?), knowing our perfect heavenly Father is pleased with us and loves us more than we love our own kids has made our love deeper and made life way more fun in this crazy transition.

The final and possibly craziest transition (because it's the most outside of the box) is the call to full time ministry as One Love Missionaries. One Love Skate started in 2006 with a slab of cement at a local church and has grown to a dynamic discipleship and evangelistic ministry impacting skaters with the One Love of Jesus all around the world in ways we never could have imagined. In 2015 we became an independent 501c3 ministry, and since that time we have worked #ShoulderToShoulder with over 40 different people who have shared our 10 1L Values and Verses on video. We have helped lead camps, preached in churches, and taken many groups into their communities for prayer walking evangelism. Also, One Love has ordered hundreds of skateboards and skate related products to create openness for conversations, but most importantly we have helped many people have 1L Conversations with their family, friends, neighbors, and co-workers by asking others "What is One Love to You?" And "Who is Jesus to you?" Our prayer is to have 1L Reps being a positive presence in the skate community by leading Life Groups and 1L Discipleship at every skatepark in the world.

This crazy transition included breaking my foot in my mid-twenties. With a broken foot, God challenged me to love skaters more than I love skateboarding. Then he proceeded to use me to do better things for skateboarding with a broken foot than I could have with two perfectly working feet! My broken foot helped me to overcome fear and type up a gospel tract and several conversation cards. Around that time, I was given opportunities to preach in several large churches in Hawaii and North Carolina, and the platform led to many hearing the message and adding their unique abilities and resources to the ministry.

In 2015, after close to 8 years serving with a great church in Maui, God moved us for a growth season in NC to get One Love rolling--- but when he called us to move, He miraculously provided skateboard ramps the very day we had decided to move 4500 miles away (https://youtu.be/TTzjVC4_1zc). We have been so encouraged by the people, churches, and organizations who believe in One Love Skate enough to support it with their prayers and finances, and God has shown us amazing things through One Love Skate all around the world.

Recently, God has called me to be the Life Groups / Discipleship Pastor at Waipuna Chapel which lets me continue the calling God put on my life to serve as a Pastor at a local church. Nicole has taken on a significant role for One Love Skate, and we are constantly reminded not to doubt in fear but have faith. Something my friend Josh Knipple has recently helped me see, is that as we follow God through all the transitions he brings into our lives, it's almost as if Jesus is in heaven saying: "Trust that I have a higher purpose for you! Enjoy the ride—I've got this. Be creative in the transitions! The galaxies are in my palm (Isaiah 40:12)! SHAKA!" 2000 years ago Jesus Christ spoke timeless words recorded for us in John 10:10 -"The thief comes only to steal and kill and destroy. I came that they may have life and have it abundantly." Let's not let fear steal, kill, and destroy the life that Jesus wants us to enjoy. This transition to full time ministry with One Love Skate has been all-consuming at times, but we have seen many experience the One Love of Jesus, which makes it all worthwhile.

In conclusion, even though life can be full of difficult transitions (just this past week many close to us have been enduring the gamut of difficulty including physical sickness, financial pressure, and the loss of loved ones), I'd like to propose a "higher" axiom for these tough transitions than Hollywood's perspective. This higher axiom will ring true in all of our lives if we choose to live the One Love of Jesus:

"Fear can lead us to faith, and faith in the 1L of Jesus will bring true freedom."

As we live empowered by faith instead of floundering in fear, even when transitions and our daily circumstances are scary, may each of us have the encouragement we need today to drop in, enjoy the ride, and learn to love crazy transitions.

About: Joshua Marburger is a Pastor in Hawaii and Founder of the international discipleship ministry "One Love Skate" 501c3. He and his wife, Nicole, have been enjoying the ride together since meeting at North Greenville University in 2007 where they were first resourced and equipped to be "shoulder to shoulder with soldiers for the Kingdom." They now have three boys and enjoy serving, speaking, and writing to help many experience the One Love of Jesus (1L). They work hard to provide resources to help as many people as possible #LiveOneLove as a positive presence in their communities through Life Groups and Discipleship. Joshua & Nicole's prayer and passion in life is to help resource and equip disciples (1L Reps) to lead life groups at every skatepark in the world.

*Day 11*

# Hey! Look Here!

*Therefore, since we are surrounded by such
a great cloud of witnesses, let us throw off
everything that hinders and the sin that so easily
entangles. And let us run with perseverance the
race marked out for us, fixing our eyes on Jesus.*

HEBREWS 12:1–2

You hear a voice, "Hey! Hey, you! Josh! Look here! Are you listening to me? Are you hearing anything I am saying?" Suddenly you snap out of it: "Oh, yeah, I heard everything; sorry, I was just a little distracted." Seems like a common conversation when riding in the car with my wife, Lindsey. I get distracted way too easy and am oblivious to life at times.

Distractions happen in life. Whether in the form of a new girl walking by, or a TV commercial coming on, or even a child screaming—distractions are all around us. Maybe you have other things in your life that distract you, but I believe it is truly one of the greatest tools of the enemy. Hear me out.

The enemy is saying, "Fine, if I can't have your salvation, I am going to distract you from what God has in store for you," and he is subtle in the way he does it. He isn't holding up flashing signs saying, "Hey, Josh, so you know, I am going to distract you now." He is clever, he is sneaky, and he will go to every extreme to refocus your eyes away from Jesus. Yesterday we looked at Peter walking on water. Here Peter is out on the water, doing the impossible, walking on water, and then what happened? The waves around him took his eyes away from where they needed to be. Distractions! At their finest. For Peter, the waves, the fears, and the others in the boat got the best of him, and he began to sink.

In Hebrews 12:1, the author tells us to "throw off everything that hinders us and the sin that so easily entangles." There are certain areas in each of our lives where we know we get distracted easily. For a teenage guy, most of the time this distraction comes in the form of a girl (and vice versa). Think about it. Here you are, listening to a speaker, totally zoned in, and then the new girl (or guy) comes walking right in front of you. What happens? You go from totally focused to distracted in a split second, and then maybe your buddy beside you makes a comment and you lose your focus entirely. We know it happens.

I wish I could sit here and tell you that as you get older distractions go away or get easier, but they don't. To be honest, they seem to get more challenging. For example, if I truly want to spend some time in prayer, like focused prayer, I have to go to the church. If I stay in my house, I start to look around at all the housework that needs to be done. I start to notice all the renovations, or I turn on the TV. That is just me; maybe it is something different for you. The same is true for all of us, though—distractions happen.

What are we supposed to do then? Let's look back to the book of Hebrews. First off, identify what is distracting you. Throw it away; get rid of it. Like I said, for me it means leaving the area that is distracting me. I know things in my house take up my focus, so I have learned to leave them. The author doesn't just mean setting it to the side so that you continually look at it; he says to throw it off. I picture a quarterback totally launching it. Go to extremes to keep clear of these obstacles. Finally, fix your eyes on Jesus. Sound familiar? Maybe it is something to think about. Hmmm. Maybe God is saying, "Hey, pay attention to this!" Going back to the story of Peter and the waves, it's same type of idea: focus on Jesus. For each of us, this idea of focus will look different, but the idea is the same: it has to be on Jesus.

What are the things in life that distract you? Be honest.

When do you find yourself the most easily distracted?

What does it mean for you to refocus on Jesus?

What if these distractions are going to keep you from skydiving with Jesus?

Is it worth it to get rid of them and to refocus on Him?

# Day 12

## Praying

*And pray in the Spirit on all occasions with*
*all kinds of prayers and requests. With*
*this in mind, be alert and always keep*
*on praying for all the Lord's people.*

EPHESIANS 6:18

I was just thinking about a really good Christian pickup line to use on my wife when she gets back from the store. Yes, she is my wife, but when you get married, you got to act like you are still dating sometimes to make it even more fun. I am an odd human…anyway, so maybe I will jump out of a tree, and she will fall, and then I will pick her up and say, "Did it hurt when you fell from heaven?" It's funny because she fell and the whole thing about falling from heaven. Get it?

My point here is that in order to have a relationship with anyone, there needs to be good communication. Communication is key, and those of you who are serious with a boyfriend or girlfriend should start working on good communication now. There are so many ways to communicate these days. The Internet, apps, phones, e-mails, hand gestures that people give on the highway, and talking face-to-face, among other ways.

One of the things that is lacking these days because of all the technology in that list is the effort it takes to really get to know someone. Most of the time, we see families sitting around the dinner table these days, and everyone is on their iPhones. We live in a culture where everyone wants connection quickly and easily. The problem is that relationships take a lot of work. Relationships take effort and genuine care for the other person. We need to let the other person know that we can listen and desire to know where he or she is coming from. If we are always talking, then we can't really ever get to know the person we are speaking to. Great communication starts with being selfless. If you are selfish, chances are there is not a lot of good communication going on with those you care about. It might seem like there is, but what are you comparing it to?

Have you ever been at a party or a social event that you didn't want to be at? Well, I have. I'm not the type of person who likes to spend time at a place where there are a billion people, and everyone is trying to figure out what to say to the next person and wondering why we are all there in the first place. So there have been multiple times when I have walked into a room pretending to be doing something so no one would talk to me because I didn't really have anything to say. I am horrible, I know. I would, like, walk around and play with napkins or fake read, things like that. There's always that one person who gets you, though. "Hey, Chad!" Dang. "Hey, man, I'm building a swan with the napkins, and this is important." "Ha, ha, Chad, you're a funny man. So listen, have you seen the new four-wheeler from Jimmy Cracks Corn 'R' Us?" During the whole conversation, I find myself drifting off mentally. I'm thinking thoughts like, "Bro, you have something in your teeth. I wonder if *Tiny House Hunters* is on tonight? Should I get a tattoo on my face like Mike Tyson?" This is why I stay away from conversation a lot of times, because I don't like feeling fake. I want to be all in on whatever I do. I'm still working on being selfless at social gatherings.

My point is that in those situations, I am thinking something else or looking at my phone, and the other person might be doing the same. Good communication takes all parties involved being all there. I need to put aside how I feel in the moment and to situate my mind to care about the person in front of me. In relationships, I need to make time to hear the other person's heart, or I'll never get to know him or her. When it's someone you really care about, there are times we need to get away from the crowd and to hear what is really going on in order to let the person know that he or she matters. They deserve our full attention. We would want the same.

It is like this with God. Instead of praying or asking God to nourish our bodies with a ten-thousand-calorie hamburger, let's pray for real. Let's be all there. If you need a way to start, then use the A.C.T.S. method:

**Adoration:** Give God praise and honor for who He is as Lord over all.
**Confession:** Honestly deal with the sin in your prayer life.
**Thanksgiving:** Verbalize what you're grateful for in your life and in the world around you.
**Supplication:** Pray for the needs of others and yourself.

The most important thing is that you realize who you are talking to. The God of the universe! The One who created you and is allowing you to breathe right now. The One who holds the stars in the sky and knows how many hairs are on your head. (I have zero hairs…maybe you have more.) You need to learn to get away where nothing is going on and to let God know how much you adore Him and to thank Him for letting you experience this life. You need to be all there when you talk to God. By the way, God already knows everything you have done and thought. Do not be afraid to confess those things to God that are difficult. He wants you to. He wants your dirty, your bad, and your nasty because He can make you whole. He can give you peace. You are not going to offend God. He already died for it all. Now He just wants to hang out and talk with you. Many times we mess up, and we stop praying because we feel like failures. The point is that God already knows we are failures and screw-ups. That's what makes this so awesome. Ask Him to forgive you in His name, and it is done. If you are mad, tell Him you are mad. If you are mad or upset *at Him*, tell Him. Get it out. Isn't it better to talk to Him than to not talk at all? He is God; He can take it. He is the greatest counselor you could ever have and the only confidant you ever truly need.

Think about the face of Jesus and what He looks like in your mind. Talk to the person...Jesus Christ. You don't need a walkie-talkie or an app; just know you are in His presence, and you will be able to talk to your creator.

Stay in the Word, and when you don't know what to pray about, just think on the name of Jesus. Think about the fact that everything that has ever been created is under the authority of that name. Jesus is awesome! Take a note card and write down one verse to think about throughout your day. You talk to yourself anyway, might as well tell yourself God's Word. He loves you. He loves you. He loves you! Always keep that in mind!

What keeps you from having real, raw conversations with God?

Why do you think adoration comes first in the A.C.T.S. method for prayer?

Spend some time having a real conversation with God. Put away your electronics and anything else that could distract you, and sit in God's presence and converse with your heavenly Father. What was your experience like when you did this?

*Day 13*

# Skate for Christ

*So whether you eat or drink or whatever
you do, do it all for the glory of God.*

1 Corinthians 10:31

So when Chad and I were coming up with a list of topics, we wanted to discuss and include what was relevant for today's Christian. Based on that, we decided we needed a day on worship. As we split up the days and tried to work through who was taking this one, it honestly kept getting overlooked. Whether that has to do with the fact that neither of us can sing or play an instrument, or just mere coincidence, who knows, but I ended up with it. So here goes, and I hope I do it justice.

As I thought about this topic, and where to even start, I kept drawing a blank. So here is what I came up with. I thought about this question in relation to the show *Family Feud*. Here you are standing in front of Steve Harvey, squaring off with another family, and the pressure is all on you. Your palms are sweaty, and the pitters are growing under your arms in anticipation of what he will ask. "We have polled one hundred people: What is the first word that comes to mind when you think of worship?" What is your answer? Today I want to cover a few words that I believe encapsulate worship.

## God

Who would have thought that I would start here? That our worship is about God. You may be sitting there going, "Well, thanks, Josh, for pointing out the obvious to me," but hear me out. In today's modern worship in many places, we truly have started to focus on the person leading the worship instead of on God himself. Follow me here. I used to travel all the time as part of the skate ministry, seeing and listening to all types of Christian bands. It hit me personally like a brick across the side of the head as we would make our way to stage after stage, listening to these top-notch bands, God saying to me, "Josh, what if I was standing on the other hillside teaching and building relationships; would you go see the band or would you come to be at my feet?" Why it hit me so hard at the moment is because I was in a spot in life where I would say, "But, Jesus, we are talking Skillet or Tomlin, and we are singing about you. Doesn't that count? I'll be back after the show is over!" He looks right at me, confused, saying, "I am right here. You can spend time with me, God of the universe, and you are choosing to go sing about me instead?" I was broken; the reality was that I was more focused on the band than I was on God Himself. Then, of course, Lecrae happened to be playing, and I would have thought it was just God's way of truly getting the point across. (I've learned God has a sense of humor.) The song "Background" comes on...read these lyrics:

*I could play the background*
*'Cause I know sometimes I get in the way*
*So won't You take the lead, lead, lead?*

Now, in this song, Lecrae is talking about God taking the lead in his life, but these lyrics hit me differently that day. Already thinking about whether I am truly worshiping God or the musician, I started thinking about it another way. Imagine this with me... daydream with me a little bit...right in the middle of a sold-out show, as everyone is singing along to this song, "I could play the background," the music cuts out, and Jesus Himself comes walking out on the stage and begins to speak. Would you in that moment boo Him off the stage and tell Him you want Lecrae back, or would you bow down and worship Him? What would you do? I say all this not to beat you up but because I have been battling this myself, truly thinking about it. Is worship to you truly about *God*?

*Oh come, let us worship and bow down; let us kneel before the LORD, our Maker* (Psalm 95:6).

As I am writing this, another perfect analogy is happening in our world, a once-in-a-lifetime-type event. People are going crazy over it, taking off work, traveling thousands of mile to see it. If you go on Facebook, it is the craze everyone is talking about. Literally, this afternoon our world will come to a halt over this event. No, I am not talking about LeBron or TayTay coming to town; I am talking about the solar eclipse. Yes, it is a phenomenon, an incredible thing, but hear me when I say this: it is still an event made by the Creator, God Himself. Now, if I told you that on this day, at this time, God Himself wants to spend time with you or meet with you, do you think people would be taking off or traveling to His location? Hate to say it, but probably not; we would probably have some excuse or tell Him maybe later. Are you following me? We worship the created many times over the creator, taking for granted who He truly is and the fact that He wants a relationship with us. What are you worshiping today?

## Music

A second answer that I believe we would all chime in with would be music. These two words, *worship* and *music*, in church and among Christians, go hand in hand. When someone says, "I love that churches worship," what they are really saying is "I love their music." Did you know that most of today's worship music goes directly back to Scripture? That when you are singing at the top of your lungs with your hands raised high, you are actually reciting Scripture right back to the author of Scripture himself? We give worship leaders a ton of credit by saying, "Man, I love that song" or "That song put God in a whole new light for me." Did you ever realize that it is causing you to think more about God or to see God in a new light because He wrote it as His love story for you? He wants you to know Him, as we discussed in our day on the Bible…this just reinforces that idea. Next time you are in worship, take the time to read through the words instead of just mumbling along or taking the lyrics for granted. Take the time to study them, to see what God is saying to you personally, and then shout it back to Him. Worship is one of our ultimate connections with Him. One final aspect of the musical part of worship I want to touch base on is to pray before you worship that God would convict your heart with one of the song lyrics. I have personally been in services before where the worship actually challenged me and convicted me more than the message itself.

*All the earth worships you and sings praises to you; they sing praises to your name* (Psalm 66:4).

## Life

The third and final word I believe would be up on that *Family Feud* board is *life*, and it is the reason for the title of this section. I believe your life is one of the greatest forms of worship. Worship goes beyond the walls of a church, beyond having a guitar and a bunch of people singing together. Worship, at its core, is truly about connecting your heart to God's.

You may have read the title for the day, "Skate for Christ," and thought to yourself, "Scripture doesn't say that, but in my

own Josh Knipple understandable, everyday translation, it does."
Colossians 3:17 says, "Whatever you do, whether in word or deed,
do it all for the glory of God." Put on your thinking cap now.
Let's break this verse down as simply as possible. What does the
statement "whatever you do" mean? *Whatever* could mean skating, snowboarding, biking, playing guitar—anything, right?
"Whether in word or deed" is pretty straightforward, not much
translation needed: in your actions or in what you say. Now, probably the most important phrase of the verse is "do it all for the
glory of God," or do it in a way to worship and honor God. Do it
in the absolute best way you possibly can. Give it your all in a way
that points to Him. I believe this is so key, and the reason I am
so passionate about it is because I have been around a ton of kids
who feel bad that they are no good at music or can't keep a beat
or sing on key, and because of that they feel they have nothing to
offer in worship. Maybe that is you, maybe it isn't, but I would
ask you either way to give it your all. In everything! Let your life
be your worship! Like you are performing for God and for Him
alone.

Finally, in closing, worship is about *you* connecting to *God*.
Not the person beside you or what he or she is doing. It is not
about if they are raising their hands or who is distracting you or
the cute girl three rows down. Worship—whether in song, in life,
in your words, however you worship—is about you and your relationship to Him. The most authentic worship I have ever experienced was at University Baptist Church, David Crowder's church,
and not because it was him. It was so authentic because every
light in the place was out, pitch black, so you couldn't even see

the person standing right beside you. Instead of looking around and seeing who else is around and letting them affect how you worship, look up. A moment of truly connecting, with no distractions, with the God of the universe.

What does the word *worship* mean to you?

Honestly, are you more focused on those around you, on the worship leader, or on God?

What area of your life can you look at now as a form of worship after reading this?

## Day 14

## Tell em All!

*I tell you, whoever publicly acknowledges
me before others, the Son of Man will also
acknowledge before the angels of God. But
whoever disowns me before others will be
disowned before the angels of God.*

*LUKE 12:8–9*

*However, I consider my life worth nothing to me;
my only aim is to finish the race and complete
the task the Lord Jesus has given me—the task
of testifying to the good news of God's grace.*

*ACTS 20:24*

"Lexi, did you just fart?" "Ha, ha, ha! Yes, I did." That was my seven-year-old's response to me smelling something that almost ended my life and prompted my question. She was all too happy to let us know what she had done to burn my nose hairs. She is one of those people who absolutely craves attention in any way she can get it. Not everyone is like that, and in many cases, people don't like attention. That is such a weird thought, considering we are so driven by social media. We absolutely love for people to see us on Instagram or Tweetiebook or all the other social apps. We go to the bathroom and post pre–nose-hair-trimming pics. People get in front of the mirror and do forty-seven thousand push-ups, and then post before-and-after workout pics.

I started thinking about this, and it made sense. It is easy to post things when you don't have to see people face-to-face. We feel more secure because we can hide if it doesn't go so well. Yet when we are at school, we feel the need to do the "in" thing, or at least what our friends are doing. We want to be normal and liked, and everyone seems to have their version of normal. What if the true normal is supposed to be abnormal? Abnormal means deviating from what is normal or usual, typically in a way that is undesirable or worrying. In order for us to look like Jesus and to feel close to Jesus, our normal has to change. Jesus calls us to be selfless, not selfish. How selfish is it when Christians do not tell their friends about the greatest thing in the history of mankind, the one thing that can lead them out of hell and straight into eternal bliss with Jesus? We tell our friends about everything else, but when it comes to Jesus, we hide. We don't want them to not like us. Think about what we are saying to them. We are saying, without words, I would rather you like me than you spend eternity with Jesus. I am not trying to make anyone feel bad, but this really isn't about our feelings. It is about what is real and true. Please take a moment to think about what I just wrote. Let it sink in. We wonder why people don't want to live for Jesus; it's because we are cowardly most of the time. People want to know that this Jesus will change them.

If you remain the same as your friends, they will not want Jesus because they don't see anything different. *We* have to live this life in light of eternity and not in complacency. We talked about obeying God and what that looks like. Ask yourself what matters to you the most. Following Jesus or being liked by a friend? Are they your friends if they make fun of you for loving someone? Are they your friends if they judge you for having a relationship with God? Jesus is calling you to share the Gospel with everyone. He is the greatest thing for everyone, and if you love the people in your life, you would give them the best thing they could have.

Your story is the best tool you have to share the Gospel. You don't have to walk up to someone and scream, "Jesus heals you!" Dude, I would run too. But everyone has a story. You don't have to have killed people or almost committed suicide or whatever to have a great story with Jesus. Your story could be that everything was pretty good but you just felt like you were missing something. I found out that Jesus died for me and rose again, and now I can't shut up about it. We lie to ourselves and believe we can't or we shouldn't. The only power a lie has over you is if you believe it. Why don't you be the trendsetter, the one who is living his or her own beliefs in a world that tells us to do what you want anyway? Tell 'em all! Tell 'em about how insanely loving our God is and what is coming for those who are His. Tell them about Jesus!

Have you ever shared your testimony with someone? Take the time now to write out the turning points you've experienced throughout your life, and look for God's hands in each of these things.

Why do you think we're so leery to talk about Jesus to the people who are (usually) the closest to us?

Pray for God's help in ridding yourself of these fears of not fitting in or not being liked by those around you. Pray for strength to live a bold life that lives out the Gospel. Write out your prayer here.

*Day 15*

---

# You Want Pizza!

*Do not conform any longer to patterns
of this world, but be transformed bu
the renewing of your mind.*

*-ROMANS 12:2*

*Pizza! Hot and fresh with melted cheese! Bacon
and pepperoni and all your favorite toppings.
Stuffed crust! Breadsticks with marinara sauce!*

*Steak marinated in teriyaki! Perfectly
grilled to medium well! Corn on the cob.
Baked potato with all the toppings.*

*And for dessert, a Dairy Queen Blizzard!*
*Cookie dough or cookies and cream! Hot*
*chocolate syrup! Ice-cream cake!*

You getting hungry yet? You may not have been before you started reading this, but don't feel bad if you need to put the book down now and go get something to eat. Is your stomach growling? Pizza! Steak! Ice cream! Dang it, now I'm making myself hungry. What the heck did I write that for? Give me a few minutes; I'll be back to finish this thought...

Did you ever take the time to think about why you respond and react to things the way you do in life? What makes you tick? Have you ever really thought about it?

Did you know that there is a multi-billion-dollar industry out there where the entire job is to come up with ways to program people's minds to respond in certain ways? Companies will spend millions of dollars for a thirty-second commercial during the Super Bowl. Did somebody say Doritos or Budweiser? It is all about programming the mind. You may think you have control over your own life, but that is exactly what these ads are designed to do: program your mind with subtle subliminal messages. I'm loving it...how 'bout some McDonald's right now? If you could hear me right now, I am singing some theme songs from these exact commercials, and my mind has been conditioned to respond in a certain way. I say all this just to get you thinking about how easily our minds can be controlled. That was just with food. What if I just typed dollar signs throughout this day's lesson or the word *money*? Would that get engrained into your mind? Or the word *me*—me, me, me, life is all about me. See what I am saying about how easy it is for your mind to be manipulated?

The same is true of the music we listen to and the TV shows we watch. We respond in life based on what is going into our minds. What are you filling your mind with today? Growing up, I didn't understand this fact one bit; I didn't think that music, TV, and other media would have such an effect on me, but looking back, I do now. Music with explicit lyrics, Internet sites that no one should be going to, movies with scenes and images I should not have been watching—this was the crap that was filling my mind, and like the old saying goes, "what goes into your mind comes out in your life." It affected how I spoke to others and how I looked at women and even treated them. I was allowing these influences to take over me. Even beyond that, though, these influences made me think life was all about me, my image, my popularity, how much money I could make, and everything else I could use to build my own name up. In high school, during my senior year, is where I really saw this idea, that life was all about me, come out the most. I was the kicker for our high school football team (yeah, a real glamorous position to win girls over), but every time I would take the field for a field goal or extra point, my friends would all start chanting from the stands "Knipple, Knipple, Knipple," and my head would get built up hearing them. Now, in all reality, a lot of people probably joined in just for the sheer fun in saying my last name, and maybe even some fans from the other team were saying it also, but to me it was all about hearing my name, and I loved it—even beyond that, I craved it. Through music and TV, the world had programmed me to think that life was all about me, and I didn't even know it. Now I am not saying that I believe legalism is the way to go and that you should never listen to or watch these things, but for me, I allowed them to take over who I was. Years and years of this programming was now coming out in my life. Maybe as you are reading this, you are thinking this is you as well. So how do you change it?

> *Do not conform to the pattern of this world, but be transformed by the renewing of your mind* (Romans 12:2).

First off, you have to acknowledge that there are areas of your life that the world has programmed—confessing it, actually acknowledging the person you have become, and getting to the point of saying enough is enough. I'm tired of the person I have turned into. Maybe it is your language, maybe the way you look or treat others, or maybe it is the way you spend your time. The first step, though, like I said, truly has to be acknowledging the pattern you are living. When you do, cry out to God in all honesty, "I'm tired of this area of my life. Help me to get rid of this crap." See this area of your life as it is—garbage, filth, and sin. Something that you are so tired of it truly makes you sick. You can't even stand the thought of going back to it.

It is one thing to say it, though, and it is another thing to actually reprogram your mind and get rid of it in your life. Solomon says it this way in Proverbs 26:11: "As a dog returns to its vomit, so a fool returns to his folly." I know that might sound disgusting, and it may even make you nauseous reading that this it is how we are described when we return to that sin, that pattern of this world. You know it's worldly, you know it's sin, yet you continue to go back to it. Why? You haven't filled your mind with something else. You haven't filled that void, so you return to what you know.

Please listen to me here: it doesn't happen overnight; it takes time. Start to fill those areas of your life with Scripture. Start posting verses all around you to read throughout the day to fill your mind. For me it meant writing passages on note cards and posting them all around me. In the shower even (I know it might sound weird, but it's where I start my day), post it with clear tape, and allow Scripture to be the first thing to fill your mind. Put a Post-it in your car by the speedometer, or put a few in your school locker. Put verses up everywhere because the more you read them, the more you fill your mind with truth. Instead of looking at a girl in lust at school, now your mind is filled with "I will not look lustfully after a girl." How about this, if you struggle with fear, you post, "Do not fear, for the Lord your God is with you." You want to know how to reprogram your mind and fill it with the truth of Scripture. By doing this, you will slowly see your mind and your life being transformed to the ways of God.

*Then you will be able to test and approve what God's will is—his good, pleasing and perfect will* (Romans 12:2).

Finally, as you reprogram, take this verse seriously. I don't need to add anything to it. Paul was a pretty wise man, so I will allow his words to finish off this idea. Now go eat some pizza!

What are you filling your mind with?

In what ways do you believe that the world is trying to program you?

What steps will you take in changing it?

# Day 16

---

# Identity

*I have been crucified with Christ. It is no longer I
who live, but Christ who lives in me. And the life
I now live in the flesh I live by faith in the Son
of God, who loved me and gave himself for me.*

GALATIANS 2:20

Welcome back! Right now, as I write this, my own life is going through a radical transformation. Much of it is because of the topic we are on today. When I was young, I wanted to be like two people: Raphael from the Teenage Mutant Ninja Turtles and my dad. Raphael was rebellious and strong. He was tough and cool. He kicked bad-dude tail, and I thought it would be cool to walk around in first grade with my ninja red bandana and a fake *sai*, which is like his small sword. Leonardo had a bigger sword, but that is an entirely separate issue, one that can lead you in many directions. You might need to stop and get saved right now…you sinner. Just kidding.

My daddio was my hero. Still is. I looked up to him, literally and figuratively. He was like those sappy songs that talk about being bigger than life and all that jazz. He grew up living somewhat on his own from an early age and got into fights. He always tried to be loyal and would fight for his friends and family physically and by just plain ol' being there for them. He was an extremely hard worker who grew up with a dad who could punish pretty harshly, but things were a lot different back then. My grandpa is a pretty cool dude who loves Jesus too. My dad would always stick up for my family in any and every way he could. He has always been a leader. When he spoke to my sister and me, we just knew that he was a man who would die for us at the drop of a hat.

So I grew up wanting to be so much like my father; I wanted to be a fighter and a tough guy. I wanted to talk like him and act like him, but as time went on, it started to weigh on me because I only had the reflection in appearance of who my dad was. My dad is the alpha male times ten and someone you believe could shoot lightning out of his butt or something. He was that cool and still is. He was like Optimus Prime from *Transformers* but shorter. But no matter how hard I tried, I couldn't be like him, and it made me feel bad. I wanted to be like him 'cause he was my best friend and my surf buddy. I tried so hard to walk in his shoes, it sort of made my own mind a prison, and I felt less of a young man, and even less when I became a man. It wasn't until I realized that God created me differently than He created my dad that my outlook began to change. We are both made in God's image, but we have different personalities, different gifts, and different paths. I was always looking at my dad so much that I never looked at my heavenly Father to know who I really was. I am made in the *imago Dei* (the image of God), and He called me here into this existence for a reason. God wanted me just the way I am so that I could influence this world with my idiotic personality and see everyone I know come to know Jesus and take on hell with a squirt gun if we were called to do so.

God revealed to me that my dad was in my life to help me see that I need to completely rely on Jesus. When I tried to be someone I was not, I became miserable and depressed. I got so low not knowing who I was; I even wanted to commit suicide at one point. That had nothing to do with my earthly dad, but it had everything to do with not knowing who I was in my heavenly Father. I was holding on to being rebellious and cool; being the alpha male tough guy was what I wanted. Truthfully, I am nothing like that on the inside. I tear up at *The Lion King*. Without knowing that my life is in Jesus, I was walking around dead. It affected everyone around me for years. Now I know my life is Jesus, my thoughts are Jesus, my love is Jesus, and without Him I do not want to live because I would not know who I am. So we take examples from other people, but we walk in the Holy Spirit to let the life of Jesus be shown in and through us. You are now a child of God, and you walk as a child of God because you were worth dying for. God is going to use your personality to change the world around *you*. Do not become someone you aren't; it will take you down a depressing path. Step back and write down the traits that you have in yourself. Now ask yourself, have you given who you are and the qualities you have to Jesus? You are who you are for a reason. Find yourself in Christ before you find your path is lost in someone else. You gain control when you choose to give it up to Jesus of your own free will. Then you will know who you really are.

What are the top three traits you see in yourself? What are *your* passions?

Stop and pray that God would use those traits for the good of the Kingdom in order to share His Word. What are your thoughts after praying this bold prayer?

Do you find your worth in what other people say about you or what God says about you? Explain and dive into these thoughts.

*Day 17*

---

# Don't Let Your Past Define You

*Since, then, you have been raised with Christ,
set your hearts on things above, where Christ is,
seated at the right hand of God. Set your minds
on things above, not on earthly things. For you
died, and your life is now hidden with Christ
in God. When Christ, who is your life, appears,
then you also will appear with him in glory.*

COLOSSIANS 3:1–4

*But whatever were gains to me I now consider loss
for the sake of Christ. What is more, I consider
everything a loss because of the surpassing worth
of knowing Christ Jesus my Lord, for whose sake*

# Skydiving with Jesus

*I have lost all things. I consider them garbage,*
*that I may gain Christ and be found in him.*

PHILIPPIANS 3:7–9

'm drinking coffee right now, and if you know me at all, you
would think I am loony for ingesting caffeine. Although I am
a pretty hyper dude, there are times when getting away from
everyone and everything seems like the only thing to do. To
be honest, it is a double-shot Starbucks energy coffee. Holy bat
crap, that's a lot of energy. It has guarana in it, so that's why I
said the thing about the bat. I might be thinking of bat guano.
Either way, it made me laugh. (Picture me thinking really in-
tensely right now with noise-canceling earmuffs on so that I
can't hear the *Emoji* movie in the background. #parentlife #loud
#kidsareweird.)

When you look behind you right now, what do you see?
Hopefully not a tiger chasing after you or anything but probably
a wall or something, right? Well, you may be reading this wanting
God to wave a magic wand so that your past doesn't control you
anymore. Maybe you just want to move on from it or not think
about it. You might have a friend who is struggling tremendously
with his or her own past. To be honest, as I write this, the devil
would like nothing more than to let my past distract me and drag
me down so that this message doesn't get to you. That will not
happen. Amen!

So here we go! When I was six, I saw a few movies that had naked women in them and other not-so-great action scenes. This led me as a little boy to have feelings and thoughts I shouldn't have been thinking or feeling. As I grew up, I would be plagued with where my mind wanted to go, as many young men are, but I had dealt with it far too young. By the time I was a teen, I felt shame and was disgusted with myself. My parents raised us in a very moral house, but as you know, everything starts in the mind. Porn became a part of my life and had a hold on my mind. Many, many young men and women are dealing with this right now. I had even lied about having sex at an early age to my friends so that I could be cool and fit in. The weight kept piling on. I started lying to my parents about smoking weed and partying.

The weight of my lies, my thoughts, and my drinking began to turn me into something I was not. Truthfully, I didn't know who I was or whose I was. Praying the prayer didn't change me. When I found out that Jesus had things to say to me, I began to listen. When I applied them, it changed little by little. It was my decision to follow Jesus and not just want a get-out-of-hell-free card that changed me. The truth is this didn't happen until late in life when I really decided not to let my past define me. If you are dealing with thoughts that keep you up at night, if you feel enslaved or like you are a prisoner in your own mind, whatever you have done in your past, I want you to know there is not a way out but a way through!

We need to live in the present. Your past is your past, so leave it there. We have talked about reprogramming the mind, and when you desire to replace thoughts or habits, it takes effort and discipline. Right now you have to decide you will not be defined by a mistake, a failure, or anything else from your past. Your life can tell a story of victory because it's not how you start but how you finish. There will always be something or someone trying to drag us down, but when you have a victor's instead of victim's mentality, you can overcome! There will be moments you doubt yourself. These moments haven't come to stay; they have come to pass.

Today, right now, you will decide to live in the present and to overcome past desires. Not tomorrow, not a year from now—today. If your real desire is to have victory, then claim it and start living it in Jesus's name. You need to adjust your current desires to fit the desires of Jesus Christ for your life. Today your primary focus will be to learn to love God and to love others. When this is your desire, it's hard to focus on your past mistakes or the things that have happened to you. Slowly, as you put the word of God in your heart, you become what God says you are. So fix your desires on Jesus in the present.

You need to start having the right view of God. Your past does not define God, so you shouldn't let your past define God in your mind. God cannot lie. If He says He loves you, He does. If He says you are forgiven, then walk in that thought. So think on that. Focus on the character and person of Jesus Christ and not on yourself. When we focus on ourselves, then we are focusing on imperfection. If you want victory and peace, then focus on the one who is those things. My character and yours are flawed.

When I think about Jesus and His past on earth, it is hard to focus on my own past. He lived, died, and rose again so that I could be free of my past. Don't be chained by things that aren't even there.

You must identify the way you talk and think about your past difficulties and ask God to forgive anything that is not of Him. Have you developed bad habits because of your past—a life of sex, drugs, alcohol, bullying, and so on? If you have, then ask for forgiveness and know that God will forgive you and cleanse your heart so that it will not be hard. This is the time to fess up where we mess up! This way you can go to God with a pure heart and feel His presence. That being said, if you have been abused or raped, or have gone through something else that was traumatizing, please do not hesitate to ask for help. Asking for help is a sign of a strong person.

God forgives and wants to move on with you, so it isn't God who has the issue of forgiving. It's you and me. Forgive yourself. You will not let your life be defined by your past. You will set your mind on Jesus, who is coming again, and you will be defined by everything He says you are. Your identity is in Jesus. Not your parents or a mistake or a troubling thought. You are the King's kid. *Learn* from the past but *live* in the present.

> *"Life is like a wave. You can't change the way it breaks, but you can change the way you ride it."*
> —Anonymous

When you look back on your past, do you feel shame, condemnation, and the like? Do you wish you could go back and change the past? Explain.

Read Philippians 3:13–14, and rest in the thought that God makes a way for us to put our past where it belongs: in the past. Express your thoughts here.

What does it mean to you to know that when God looks at you, He doesn't see a tainted past but rather His precious child?

*Day 18*

---

# Stabbed In The Back

*If anyone slaps you on the right cheek,*
*turn to them the other also.*

*-MATTHEW 5:39*

Have you ever been hurt in your life? Like really hurt, stabbed in the back, talked about by someone you thought you could trust? Have you ever been let down by someone failing you or falling through on a promise? If you are breathing right now as you read this, then the answer is without a doubt *yes*. We all have been hurt at some point in our lives, some worse than others, but it happens even to the best of us. Others let us down, and we let others down; it is part of life. I hate to say it, but it will happen again at some point. I don't write this to bring you down or to put you back into that spot of pain; I bring it up because I believe how we respond goes a long way in seeing God move in our lives. We are called to forgive, and that is exactly what we are going to focus on here today: forgiveness.

*Be kind and compassionate to one another, forgiving each other, just as in Christ God forgave you* (Ephesians 4:32).

Do you see that key factor there, that final phrase that Paul writes in his letter to the Ephesians? Forgive just as Christ God has forgiven you. Let's take a moment to really think about that. What if we used the same standard in forgiving others that God uses in forgiving us? Unconditionally, no strings attached, arms spread wide open. Christ went to the cross to offer us forgiveness. What if we understood the lengths God went to to restore our relationship with Him? Jesus went to the cross to forgive you! Getting the picture yet? You are meant to forgive! Instead of just taking my word for it or just one verse, we look at Christ's teaching in modern terms (see Matthew 18:22–35).

Here it is, your senior year, and prom is coming up. You want to impress your date but not only her—you want to leave others speechless. You want to be the talk of the evening. Just so happens that as prom season rolls around, you see someone pull into church in a brand-new, bright-red, eye-popping Lamborghini. We are talking one of a kind. So you work up the courage to ask if you can use it for your big night. To your surprise, the owner agrees and tells you to have a memorable night. Prom goes off with a bang. As you pull in, everyone notices, pointing and stopping to stare. Your date even gives you a kiss on the cheek as you are pulling away from the crowd. Trying to show off a little bit, you hit the gas a little more than you realize, take the first turn too sharp, and slide right off the side of the road. After bouncing off the guardrail, you cross the center line head-on into traffic. The car is totaled. All you can think is "I am dead; he is going to kill me." You have no excuses, no way to talk yourself out of it, and you know you owe this guy big-time. Shaking as you get to his house to explain the situation, begging for forgiveness, confessing what you did, you are amazed when the man who let you borrow his prized possession looks at you and says, "You know what, I was a kid once, and I know it can happen to anyone. I forgive you." Blown away, you leave, thinking about all the mercy you have just been shown.

Monday morning comes around, and you are back to driving your old clunker of a car into school; talk about a difference from Friday night. As you are pulling into the parking lot, someone runs the stop sign and bumper tags you. In the heat of the moment, you get out, screaming at the tiny dent the person just left in your bumper. You call the police and get them involved to ensure the other driver pays you for every penny you can get. He apologizes over and over, yet you are adamant: no way are you going to forgive him. See the paradox here? When you really think about it, this is the scene and exactly what we do when it comes to God forgiving us and then how we respond to others. We love the idea of God's abundant grace and forgiveness, yet when it comes to passing that on, heck no. We hold on to bitterness; we hold grudges.

This is a key factor in this story that we want to overlook many times and that would be easy to gloss over. The man who forgave you for destroying his car hears that you are not willing to forgive, and he is now furious and calls you to his house. "You wicked, evil, selfish child. I forgave you everything, and you can't do the same? I gave you the example for you to follow, not to take for granted." We are to forgive just as Christ has forgiven us. Take a moment now to truly think about all the things in your life God has forgiven you for, so much more than a totaled car, beyond what you can even comprehend. Now will you go and forgive others, or will you hold on to the hurt they caused you?

Now you might be sitting there reading this and making the assumption that I have never been hurt and forgiveness comes easy to me. To be honest, I am not going to write about something I haven't had to practice myself, and I write this section with tears in my eyes. In my own life, I have had to learn forgiveness the hard way, and I am going to be very open with you here. My uncle, as we were growing up, was my brother's idol. Everything my uncle did, my brother wanted to do. Because my uncle was single, Trav wanted to be single. Because my uncle was an engineer, Trav wanted to be an engineer. Everything! During this time our entire family was extremely close; eight grandsons who were inseparable, and my uncle was always at the center of everything we did. Until about ten years ago. My uncle went to jail for life, and our family was torn to shreds because of what he did. (There are still divisions to this day.) Beyond even the divide in our family, I witnessed firsthand what it did to my brother. He was broken, and I hurt for him. I was angry, bitter, and just honestly hated what my uncle did to our family. I would have days when I would want to hug him, and I would have days when I would truly just want to punch him. As time went on, God has broken down my heart, showing me the grace that Christ offered me on the cross and convincing me that I need to do the same for my uncle. Do I always want to? Absolutely not. Do I have the strength to forgive him and visit him? Not on my own. But I know it is what God is calling me to do and that when I am weak, He will give me that strength.

Forgiveness is like a check-engine light on my heart. When I am bitter and not ready to forgive, it is God flashing in my life, saying, "Hey, something isn't right at this moment." Now you may want to ignore the check-engine light or pretend it isn't there, but God is trying to work on your heart to set you free. By holding on to bitterness and anger, you are handcuffing yourself to what that person did to you. God is saying to you, "Let it go. It is hindering what I am trying to do in your life." When you don't have that strength, pray, and God will give you the strength that Christ had to endure on the cross to forgive you.

*Father, forgive them, they know not what they do* (Luke 23:34).

One of the biggest things I have come to learn in working with others on the idea of forgiveness is this: Those who have hurt you many times don't even know that they have. Maybe it is a sarcastic remark they made that they thought was said in fun but that cut you to your core, and you can't get it out of your mind. A stray comment someone made not knowing your history of verbal abuse. Someone who let you down, and it truly was just a matter that they forgot, that they didn't mean it, but to you it was a matter of trust. Soldiers nailing Jesus to the cross, just doing their jobs, not knowing any different. See what I am saying? We are hurt so many times by others, and they may not even realize it. How will you respond? Jesus calls us to forgive.

I know this may be one of the hardest aspects of what Jesus calls us to do as believers, but I believe it can also be one of the greatest pieces of our testimony. You may be saying, "Josh, you don't know what that person did to me." Do you not realize it was your sin that put Jesus on the cross? When He was saying, "Father, forgive," I believe He was speaking directly for you and me. Forgiving the unforgivable! When you do forgive, you learn what it means to have Christ's strength, and this single act will help you to see the lengths Christ went to for you. In forgiveness there is freedom, and it will unlock a new level of what God wants to do in your life. This is such a serious matter that in Matthew 5 Jesus even goes as far as saying if you are preparing to give your sacrifice but there is division, leave the sacrifice and go and make it right. Can you imagine the number of people who should be leaving church on Sunday mornings at our worship services if we actually took this seriously? It is God's Word; maybe it is time we started to listen. To skydive with Jesus, you need to learn to practice forgiveness.

If God has placed someone on your heart during this chapter, will you forgive that person?

What if God used the same standard in forgiving you that you use for others?

If forgiveness is a check-engine light in your heart, is it flashing right now? Will you take care of it or ignore it?

*Day 19*

# Dating/Friends

*Do not be misled: "Bad company
corrupts good character."*

1 CORINTHIANS 15:33

*A friend loves at all times, and a brother
is born for a time of adversity.*

PROVERBS 17:17

So about ten minutes ago, I was watching what could have been an awesome reality show as my two-year-old was building a fort with her mother in our living room. They used a blanket and two coffee tables. Kalyssa, the two-year-old, tried to crawl into the fort through the blanket and *smack alack*, she ran into the legs of the table. Don't hate me, but that was hilarious. She just stopped and pondered how in the world the table got there. A minute later, as she is playing in the fort, we can hear her, but the blanket is keeping her out of our sight. We just hear random squeaks and other noises. She comes out from the blanket and has fake corn on the cob in her mouth and walks to her mother like a dog and spits out the fake corn into her hand. We just look at each other thinking, "She is *your* child." She runs in place for like five seconds, says, "Blah blah dada my mazing," and runs back to her fort. Kids are weird! We think she was trying to tell us how amazing we are as parents and that she couldn't be happier that she gets to share time with us. She also could have said we suck, and she wants corn on the cob. We are not sure, but she is still supercute.

Not knowing what other people are thinking or saying behind my back has been hard to deal with at times for me. I have always cared what people thought but played it off like I didn't. There are times when I wish people who didn't tell me the truth or wouldn't tell me how they felt would get "smack alacked" like Kalyssa. That doesn't sound good, but I'm just being real with you. Things like dating can be tough because we go through so many different emotions, and when we want someone to like us, there are moments when we even step outside of who we are to impress people. People tell us to follow our hearts, and to be honest, that is a little crazy when you step back and think about it. What if your heart, which can be led by pure emotion, causes you to do something destructive, or out of character, or puts you in a situation you don't want to be in? Don't allow your emotions to control you. You control them. Discipline your emotions.

Being "feeling led" is a topsy-turvy, up-and-down way of living life, and it often leads to being hurt and depressed. We need to be Spirit-led. Look around you. How many people go through hard breakups and fallouts in relationships, giving everything to a person because they felt like he or she was a hottie, which led to sexual feelings, which made them think they were in love? Many times all a person these days has to do is say "I love you," and the other person falls into a spiral of being "all in" on a situation or relationship that will destroy his or her heart. It can make you do things you started out not wanting to do. Because of this you end up hating yourself and feeling unloved, and maybe it even distorts your view of a "godly" marriage. That is dangerous because God wants you to have an awesome marriage where you share the real you and know that the other person isn't there for just feelings but is there through it all. The ups the downs and everything in between. The type of person who you can share the worst parts of you with and who will love you anyway while you both take those tough things to Jesus.

There are times in any relationship when you have bad days. Circumstances should not determine the love that you have for someone. Love is not a feeling; it is a choice. It is about sacrificing how you feel to make someone else's day or life better. Jesus is the perfect example of perfect love. We are called to love one another, which is a sacrificial type of love. Living in a way that our lives and our days are not about us. This type of love doesn't just look at someone and make knee-jerk decisions about him or her. This love wants to get to know the other person. It comes into a situation and knows that every human being is a sinner or has messed up in some way, and it accepts that. This also helps us make wise choices by not jumping into emotional decisions that can turn us into someone we are not. There is no perfect person for you in a dating relationship or friendship. There is a person who can come alongside you and help to totally rock out life with you, no matter what it throws at you.

My wife said I could use part of her story, so I'll share a little about her. When she was seventeen, she was totally into a guy who told her he loved her, and she believed him. He didn't judge her, and he let her do whatever she wanted. They had sex because she *felt* she loved him too. It turns out that he had other girls he was doing something similar with, playing with the girls' emotions to fill his emotional love tank with physical pleasure. Leah, my wife, would think the entire time that they would end up together, and it never happened. For the next ten years, it would be an emotional roller coaster of her doing drugs, partying, and using sex as a Band-Aid for how she felt on the inside.

A big part of passionate, successful living is about surrounding yourself with people who are following Jesus and lifting you up, not bringing you down. Even in a friendship, each party should not just be there to get what they want out of the deal. They should each be there for the other, adding to what the other might lack, loving when it's hard, and showing that relationships are built on respect, integrity, and putting the other person before yourself. It isn't easy, but things that are worth it usually aren't. Things that are worth it take effort. Are you putting in the effort to think about who is in your life and who might not need to be? Are you putting in the effort to be a light in your friend's life? Don't be a vacuum in the relationship with the power button on. Then you start getting used to using the other person, and just by being around you, he or she becomes emotionally drained.

In order for us to really "be all there" for any relationship, we must first learn to "be all there" with Jesus. Know who you are and live by a code, so to speak. If you date or have a friend, then that person is there to walk life with you, not run over you or change you. Walking side by side on a journey is different than having a person in your life run over you emotionally. Being Spirit-led is about being so close to Jesus that when you know a moment or thought isn't what God wants you to do, His strength is enough to guide you through or away. It's also about being courageous and being a difference-maker in people's lives, not being an emotion-taker. Be strong enough to not dry out people emotionally, and be the person who helps lead your boyfriend, girlfriend, or friend to the "living water." If you can do this, then you won't lose who you are, and your self-esteem will skyrocket. Not because of you taking from people but by giving them the real you, the real love that you can offer because of Christ changing you inside. Be courageous enough to be you! Not the person you think other people want.

While you were reading this, did someone come to mind who may not be the healthiest person to have in your life? Explain.

Why do you think it's important to have relationships that are focused on God?

Have you ever thought of relationships as being a gift from God? Why or why not? If not, has this changed?

*Day 20*

# What You Worried About?

*So do not fear, for I am with you: do not*
*be dismayed, for I am your God.  I will*
*strengthen you and help you.  I will uphold*
*you with my righteous right hand.*

*- ISAIAH 41:10*

"What was that noise? Did you hear it? Is someone in the house? Go check. You want a flashlight? What if someone broke in? Hold on, take the dog with you." What if, what if, what if? The questions started to pile up, and I could see the fear starting to take over in my wife's mind. At that point, I knew we needed to quit watching *Criminal Minds* as often as we were. Here we were, sitting on the couch, and the wind blew and knocked over a board in the attic, but in her mind it became what

I call a worst-case scenario. For me, I just started laughing (which doesn't go over well when your wife is being serious) and noticed that our one-hundred-pound dog is just lying on the floor, not even flinching about the noise, so it doesn't really concern me either. I do my best to calm my wife down, telling her that the doors are all locked and that everything is OK. The problem is by this point, the what-if questions have started taking over.

Don't worry about it! I read that time and time again in Scripture, and in my simple mind that is exactly how I would live. I wouldn't worry about anything. Ever. My mind was very basic, and I really don't let things get to me. My natural response to stressful things or worries others would have would be to start laughing. Now don't get me wrong; I was not mocking or down-playing what others were going through. It was a just a learned response I picked up on from my dad. When he goes through stressful times (which you can tell by his hair standing up), he just laughs. I don't understand worry or anxiety, at least not until the last few years. Then I got married. My wife, at times, deals with anxiety. So when I would start laughing, needless to say, it didn't go over well. So to help me write this day and address worry, as well as anxiety, I have asked her to help me understand and even discuss what some of you might be going through right now.

During pregnancy with Eli, Lindsey's anxiety spiked to the point of many sleepless/restless nights. When I say sleepless nights, I mean up for clips of three to four hours, just shaking in fear, unable to shut off a terrible thought. She said these thoughts never stopped. They caused an almost unexplainable feeling that she would do anything to get rid of. I won't go into all the details, but I will say it gave me a new perspective, even an appreciation, for those who live with anxiety or depression. I never had a clue how much it could consume someone's life and/or thoughts. All I could do was sit there, put worship on, and honestly, start reading Scripture. It was the only thing I could do to calm her mind, because everything I would say otherwise would just make it worse.

It got to a point where we actually gave a friend of ours who does Christian counseling a call. She directed us to passages that I want to share with you all in hopes that it helps as much as it did for my wife.

*Do not be anxious about anything, but in every situation, by prayer and petition, with thanksgiving, present your requests to God. And the peace of God, which transcends all understanding, will guard your hearts and your minds in Christ Jesus. Finally, brothers and sisters, whatever is true, whatever is noble, whatever is right, whatever is pure, whatever is lovely, whatever is admirable—if anything is excellent or praiseworthy—think about such things* (Philippians 4:6–8).

In my mind, when I heard the beginning of the first verse, "don't be anxious," I was like "See, Lindsey, I told you so. Just don't worry about it." Then came my humbling moment as Jen, our counselor, went on to share with us that it isn't as simple as my mind thought it was. She went on to share that the passage exists because people do deal with anxiety. If they didn't, Paul wouldn't have to address it. For me, it was one of those aha moments. Maybe I needed to learn more, like when to keep my mouth quiet and how to actually help my wife.

Then we learned that when the anxieties and worries do start coming up, no matter the situation, to pray. Take it to God. The One and Only who can overcome the thoughts in your mind. Your mind can do some crazy things and put some off-the-wall thoughts through that head of yours. However, God Himself is greater than your mind. So take it to Him. Trust that He can overcome all. I'm going to get a little blunt with you here. If our God has the power to raise Christ Jesus from the dead, I believe He has the power to calm our minds. Will you let Him? Even if you don't know what to say, just cry out.

Paul gives us the puzzle piece that maybe you have been missing: *think upon what is good.* As I addressed earlier in the book about reprogramming your mind I will say again here. Focus on whatever is good, excellent, pure, and true, and you will see what the result will be: peace!

I'll say it again: peace! That is what my wife needed and was craving as she went through these times. Peace over her mind so that she could just rest. Now this wasn't an easy overnight fix. It took practice, time, and repetition, but eventually she was able to beat her anxiety.

What is causing you to be anxious right now?

Do you believe Jesus is greater than that fear? Explain what that means to you.

What are the good things in your life you will begin focusing on instead of your fear?

# Fear to Faith Personal Testimony 2
# Cody Davenport: Worship Leader

There have definitely been more than a handful of times where I have seen God change or maybe a better word is 'refine' my fear into faith. I know one story that sticks out in large way, mainly because it changed the path my life was going. My first year of college I went to a very small school in Louisville, Kentucky. The only reason I went there was because it was ridiculously cheap, I had friends that were going there, and I didn't want to stay home to go to community college. So, I decided to go there and take my base classes knowing I would transfer elsewhere.

That year was a fun year, cause I was with my very best friends and living on my own for the first time and all that comes with that. But it definitely was not a significant time of spiritual growth. When that year ended, I sent my transcripts off to University of Louisville, got accepted, picked out my classes and was ready to go for the fall.

That summer I worked at a camp close to my hometown in Ohio. I grew up going to this camp, and I figured it would be a fun way to have a job for the summer, and I was right! I had a blast that summer. I met some lifelong friends, and one of the weeks God really kinda smacked me in the face. It was a week where we had a speaker in for the camp, who had been in South Africa as a missionary for the past 3 years. He was in his late 20s maybe early 30s. Shawn. Shawn was cool, and had some great stories but I honestly don't remember most of his sermons. What I do remember very specifically was when we were saying goodbye to him at the end of the week, it was much of the normal high fives and hugs, but he grabbed me by the arm and looked me dead in the eye and said '…listen man, God wants to use you.

He wants to do big things through you, but you have got to let Him.' I still remember the feeling I had. Kind of like grief, like I had let my spiritual life die in the past year. The next thought was, I didn't even pray about what school I should go to or what I should do this next year. And that is when the fear came.

I felt like I had made a decision and felt trapped and not sure what to do. I began to pray about that circumstance, asking God specifically what He wanted. I immediately knew it wasn't University of Louisville, but I also didn't know what was in its place. So that meant…more fear. Fear of the unknown, fear of being labeled a drop out and all sorts of other fears. But the largest one was the fear of the unknown. I mean the timeline on this was far from ideal. I was enrolled in classes that were going to start in less then 2 months, and didn't really want to take time off, but had no idea what was next.

I had visited Liberty for college for a weekend my jr year of high school and loved it, but never considered it. But it became very apparent that was where I was supoosed to go. Long story short I made the decision to try to go to Liberty in JULY, I was accepted and started that next month.

So, what's the big deal? Well, if I would have operated out of fear and not faith, I would have stayed in Louisville. I would not have met my wife, I would not have been called into ministry (at least not the way I was at Liberty), I would not have been able to travel and learn the ropes of leading worship with a worship band, and so many other things.

Hindsight is of course 20/20, but it is amazing to look back and see how much of my life and its course started with the decision to act in faith and not in fear.

*Day 21*

# Making Good Choices

*How much better to get wisdom than gold, to get insight rather than silver!*

PROVERBS 16:16

What's up, what's up, what's up! OK, so I have a funny story for you today, and if you don't laugh, then I don't care. My family and I went to the lake the other day, and it was cloudy with a chance of meatballs. (Sorry, that movie is good, though.) Well, my seven-year-old, Lexi, can't swim, and she doesn't really want to be taught, but she says she does. More on that in a second. So I have my two-year-old with her little bitty bikini on and a diaper filled with water so it looks like we haven't changed it in three weeks, which is cracking me up as she waddles around. I tell Lexi she needs to learn how to swim, and she says OK. What transpires is hilarious.

So we are in maybe a foot and a half of water, and I say, "Lexi, lie down on my arms, and we can work on moving your arms and kicking your legs." So she does, barely, and she is extremely nervous that her face is going to go under the water. I am saying, "No, it won't. You'll be fine." The entire time she didn't listen to me once and began to yell because she didn't trust me. So...I threw her about three feet away from me. LOL! She comes up yelling and hoping to get attention while she is standing in a foot of water. There are people about a hundred feet away who think she is being attacked by a great white and a T. rex at the same time. I'm telling her chill out, and she walks up on the sand where she decides not to go back in the water. If you know me then you know we face our fears in my family. So I start chasing her...LOL. She is screaming, so I start screaming, and I'm cracking up, and the people around us are cracking up as she runs around like a raptor is chasing her. I even stopped, and she ran yelling for another hundred yards or so. So I grabbed her and threw her in the water again. She decided to just let me teach her after that.

We all make decisions every day. Some good and some bad. Some of us might just need to make the choice to decide to decide. Some wander around aimlessly, metaphorically screaming, when no one is chasing them. Meaning, instead of making choices at all, we tend to drift along a path of indecision when we could have just stopped and faced this thing head-on. Drifting is dangerous. One day you could look up and be so far from where you wanted to be that it might seem hopeless to even try again. What will not happen right now is me telling you that making the right choices will make everything better. That isn't necessarily true. Life isn't fair all the time, and bad things can happen.

Success in our culture is defined many times as making money and having things. In order to do that, people will tell you to get good grades and go to college. Then get an awesome job doing something that pays well, and when you get stable, settle down with someone. We have people telling us what to do as if there is a formula for success. The question is what determines success. Is success the same for everyone? What if someone offered you millions of dollars, a superhot spouse, and a huge mansion with the whole world thinking you are awesome? Yet inside you felt like you had no purpose and went to sleep each night feeling numb. Would you take that deal?

People make great choices all the time and have bad things happen to them. People have worked hard but lost their jobs due to cutbacks. Natural disasters can wipe people's houses and belongings off the map. Making good choices does not promise success, the same as making some bad choices does not make you a failure. Instead of trying to please everyone and use their definitions of success, why not step back and think about what success is to you. If missionaries risk their lives to share the Gospel every day and have absolutely no money, are they failures? Absolutely not. They are loving others by giving people the greatest thing imaginable. They have purpose, drive, and adventure. Success is not defined by what we get or what we have but by *who* we have and *who* we get. We have Jesus, and we get to bring people to Him.

Success is not just a matter of perspective. The right perspective is looking at it like Jesus does. At the end of the day, success is about knowing your purpose and then living it out. Your purpose is to love your creator with all your heart, mind, and body while loving others as Jesus did. If you do not think that is an adventure in itself, then I dare you to travel to India and go to the slums and start sharing the Gospel. The closer you are to God, the better the decisions you will make, and some might sound crazy at times. Ladies and gents, we will not take our money and things to heaven. So why spend your whole life trying to accumulate things that you can't keep anyway? Now I am not saying money is bad and having nice things is bad. But I do want you to really think about what God has in store for you and not just the Americanized plan for success. Right now think about how many people have money and are unhappy. Look at our celebrities; it's unreal how unhappy they are. The most famous celebrities in the world continue to come out and say they don't feel loved and are depressed. Their relationships almost never last. I am not making this up. Very, very few celebrity marriages last.

You should obey your parents and listen to wise counsel, but what I am saying is that they are not you. When we make our choices based on other people's ideas of success, we start living another person's story and not our own. How many students go to the military because every man in their families did the same? How many students simply follow in the footsteps of their parents because that's all they have known from the time they were born? I am not even saying that isn't what God wants you to do. But what if? What if we are blinded by the norm but God has this extraordinary adventure if we just step back and listen to Him? Get close to Jesus. So close that your life is risky and not safe at times because you find yourself following Jesus wherever He tells you to go. Find adventure in the Lord, and be willing to step into the kind of success that brings glory to God and not to other people.

Wisdom is the application of knowledge. Just because we might know a few things does not necessarily mean we are wise. What really matters is how we apply or use the knowledge we have. Choose to make good choices. It's easy to do the wrong thing; it can be hard and might take courage to do the right thing.

How do you make major decisions? Do you make them alone? Allow other people to weigh in? Take it to God and ask for help? Explain.

What's your personal definition of success?

Do you put your value and worth into the material or the spiritual? Whatever your response, explain why your value is in that and how it affects you.

## Day 22

# I Got You Man!

*Therefore encourage one another*
*and build each other up*

*-1 Thessalonians 5:11*

"Dad, I'm scared! I don't think I can do it." This is all that was going through my mind as my five-year-old eyes stared down at the steepest ski slope I had ever seen. "You got this, my man, I believe in you," my dad replied. "But, Dad, the signs at the top all say experts only." Now I would love to sit here and tell you that the only reason I was shaking was how cold it was, but the truth is, I was scared to the point of almost peeing myself. Remember, I was only five, so give me a break. My dad believed in me and knew I could do it and was going to be my greatest supporter. "I'll buy you a Matchbox on the way home," he went on to say. Now I am not saying that you should bribe others to do things, but for my dad, he knew what it would take to conquer my fears. Even with my mom objecting in the background, I went for it. I got to the bottom of the mountain, and my dad told me to look up at what we had just conquered together. "Ahhhhh, heck yeah! I feel the need, the need for speed," I screamed. (*Top Gun*, anyone?) At that point my dad stuck out his ski pole and said, "Give me some pole!" (It's a ski thing as a way to celebrate.) My joy for skiing and living on the mountain ensued. My dad believed in me, he knew I could do it, and he was the encouragement I needed to take that first run. Ever since, I know that I have my parents in my corner to encourage me in my life.

I wanted to start out this day with a story of encouragement. As you have been reading through this book, maybe God has instilled a dream in you that you know He alone is calling you to. Maybe it is stepping out and going on a mission trip or taking a stand for the outcasts in your schools. You want to do it, you know He has called you to it, but as you share this vision with others, they always seem to be trying to talk you out of it—not only shattering your dreams but also always putting you down and bringing out the worst in you instead of the best. So today I want to discuss with you a topic that is very practical but also very personal to me: avoiding negative influences. I have seen way too many kids give up on their dreams and God-given passions because of a few negative people around them.

I will never forget my high school football team hitting the gym and lifting to prepare for the season. Coach Schleich would always believe in us and push us to lift to our potential, challenging our limits. On the other hand, though, I also remember we had a few shmucks on the team who, instead of encouraging one another, would always be the jerks, saying, "No way, you can't lift that." In those moments I had a choice to make: Who do I listen to, Coach's encouragement or the guys telling me I can't do it? As I got down on the bench to go for my personal record, I hear both sides coming at me: "You can do this" and "No way."

**Choice number 1:** I listen to those negative influences. Chances are pretty good that if I am listening to the voices saying, "No way," they are going to get inside my head, and I can pretty much guarantee failure before I take the weight off the rack.

**Choice number 2:** I listen to Coach, who is going to push me to do what he believes I can. A good coach isn't going to push me beyond what he has prepared for me and trained me to do. As I lay down on the bench, he is saying, "Remember your form, remember what I taught you. You got this."

I knew the importance of positive influences in my life and how to listen to them, so I got down on that bench and pushed that weight. Heck yeah. New personal record!

Another way to think about it is like the old cartoons, the angel and the devil on your shoulders, "You can do this" versus "You are going to fail." These ideas and analogies are true to the influences around us. What voices are you surrounding yourself with? Those who pour into you and encourage you or those who tear you and your visions apart? The company you keep will affect the outcomes in your life. You can only be strong for so long if you continue to surround yourself with those telling you the reasons you can't. Jesus is telling you, "Go, you can do this. I have prepared you and trained you for this," while the world is telling you all the reasons you can't. Negative influences can kill dreams, quenching the spirit of what God is trying to do through you.

So as we challenge you to skydive with Jesus, whatever that looks like for you, are you surrounding yourself with those who will encourage you to do it or tell you that you are nuts? Here is the thing, though, please listen to me: you are never going to experience that thrill if you don't jump outta the plane!

*Therefore encourage one another and build each other up* (1 Thessalonians 5:11).

The apostle Paul knew the importance of encouragement among the early church. As this church faced persecution, prison, and even death, he understood that for this early establishment to survive, lifting one another up was foundational. Can you imagine being part of that early church if all they ever heard within was negativity, that there was no hope, that Nero was a crazy dude and after them, and so on? Instead, Paul taught encouragement, speaking to and sharing with others what Jesus was doing in their lives and pouring into them.

Encourage or destroy. We can either lift people up or we can shatter their dreams. Same can be said for how people respond to what God is doing in your life. Are they lifting you up or knocking your knees out from under you? They might not even have to say anything to you but literally just their presence in the room is like a foul stench…such a negative aroma coming off of them. Before they walked in, everyone was upbeat and ready to go conquer Goliath, but now—dun, dun, dun—you feel you couldn't even go defeat an ant. They have that kind of vibe to them.

In my life personally, and why I truly believe the ministry has become so successful, is because I have a team around me who is encouraging. I know I have a wife to come home to who will lift me up. We may not always agree, and we may see things differently at times, but I still know that she has my back. I have friends who get excited about seeing God move, and I could name about five or six of them. It is crazy how much they influence me, because I get fired up even just talking to them. Lindsey can tell when I am on the phone with one of these guys, even hearing my voice coming through the back fence. I can't help it, there is a passion in these friendships of encouragement. They are saying, "I got you, man!" Beyond these friends I also have my parents, who are incredible people. They have a belief in me, in the ministry, and in what God is doing in the area.

When you have others around you who believe in you like I have, you are ready to fly! To go skydiving, to jump off the cliff, to storm the gates of hell! Who surrounds you?

Who do you surround yourself with?

How does each of them lift you up or tear you down?

Describe a time when you challenged and encouraged others or when you might have shattered someone's dreams.

# Day 23

## How to Stay in Awe

*Let all the earth fear the LORD; let all the
inhabitants of the world stand in awe of him!*

*PSALM 33:8*

*Therefore let us be grateful for receiving a
kingdom that cannot be shaken, and thus let us
offer to God acceptable worship, with reverence
and awe, for our God is a consuming fire.*

*HEBREWS 12:28–29*

Check this out: I was totally thinking about what I wanted to write in this section of the book, but right now I decided to put on some headphones and put it on We Are Messengers. This group has a song called "I'm on Fire," and when it comes on, I turn it way up to drown out everything so that I can get crazy with God. We have to actively find ways to stir up our faith. The world is not our true home, and it can put the wrong song in our heads. The song that needs to play is something like "God is so freaking amazing that I can't help but stand in awe of who you are!" Do it right now! Stand up and throw your hands to the sky and say, "God, You are amazing!" Give Him a spiritual high five. "God, You did all this, and I wish I could do something for You. I wish I could express the way I feel and want to feel about You in a way that would be worthy of who You are!"

We can and should have moments with God that we don't want to leave. Find ways to completely be consumed with His presence. If you have to, turn a song up louder than your negative thoughts. Be surrounded by godly things and have a moment that doesn't stop when the music does. Be so into God's presence that you want other people to know the truth; desire for those you love to feel what you felt. Listen, you don't need a song, but sometimes our hearts get hard, and we need that extra push to be slightly broken enough to let God take over. A seed can't grow until it dies. It breaks open and begins to grow. There are times when we need to die to ourselves and to be broken enough to not be about us so that we can grow. This entire thing we call life is about bringing glory to God.

Are you wondering why you don't feel His presence anymore and why you are down in the dumps? It's because the person you are now, the real you who is to be led by the Holy Spirit, is quenched and drowned when we are all about ourselves. Right now realize that it's about Him. Stir your faith up in such a way you might even cry, smile, laugh, dance, fall on your face, or simply clap your hands. We can get into an unconscious rut and not even know it. Let's break the boring cycle. David danced naked because he was so pumped up about God. Don't do that…unless you are in your room and doors are closed, LOL, 'cause they might lock you up afterward…but everything you are, body and soul, is His anyway.

Sometimes we have moments when we need to ask God to *take* what we feel like we can't give to Him. You might be in a place where you are saying to yourself that you have to be tough in this area or keep this part of you, even though it's not good. Maybe you have been hurt, and you feel like if you let go of your pain and be vulnerable, then you are setting yourself up for a fall. Listen, those thoughts come from a place in us that is more about us than about God. That might not be easy to hear, but our Spirit-led selves know that we can get hurt at any time, and we should still choose to love when it's hard anyway.

Go grab a friend with a guitar, and sit around a bonfire singing worship songs. Make a YouTube video saying how much you love God while you are at the beach. Start a prayer group that meets at school, but make it radical. Go outside and look at the clouds in awe of how He got them to stick up there…LOL. Let your faith be active. The more you are living out your faith, the more it gets stirred up. Keep it about Jesus, though. Don't ever lose sight of that. Even doing ministry-oriented things can become an idol if it doesn't have Jesus at the center. Stay connected to the source at all times. When you unplug your cell phone charger from the wall, it starts to lose battery. Do not unplug from Jesus. Constantly step back and see if you have unwittingly moved away from your life source. If you have…plug back in!

So give it all away. If you have to, just start with moments. Take now, for example. Why wait? What is the point of putting off something until tomorrow that can radically change you today? In this moment it can be just you and God. That is an insane thought! Are you catching on to the theme here? It's now; it's not later. Your life doesn't wait, and if you keep putting things off, before you know it, twenty years will pass. You will be looking around, like many do, and just be floored that all it would have taken was one moment of giving God time when you didn't feel like it. Listen, usually it's those times when you don't feel like it that God blesses that time with a breakthrough.

Feelings are up-and-down emotions, but God is unwavering in the flood of emotions and situations we go through. He is the lighthouse; He is the anchor that we need in the midst of the storm. So whether you are in the middle of an actual storm, a metaphorical one, or just having a normal day, step back from your routine, stand up and throw them hands up, and praise God like it's your last chance. We are not promised tomorrow, but we have now. You are only able to take the next breath because God allows it. Every day can seem ordinary and like a revolving door, and I say we make a change. So in an unordinary day, let the next breath glorify Him in an extraordinary way. Stir up your faith today and every other day!

What are some things you can do today to get away from all your distractions and just be in God's presence?

What do you need to ask God to take away from you?

What are some ways to ensure that you are staying plugged in to the life source of God?

*Day 24*

# Overcome Your Fear

*Have I not commanded you? Be strong
and courageous. Do not be afraid; do not
be discouraged, for the LORD your God
will be with you wherever you go.*

*JOSHUA 1:9*

*When I am afraid, I put my trust in you. In God,
whose word I praise—in God I trust and am
not afraid. What can mere mortals do to me?*

*PSALM 56:3–4*

Are you ready for breakthrough? Ohhhhh yeahhhhh! This topic has driven me to such a point that I had thought about ending my life. I know that is a very intense way to start today out, but in all seriousness, I have such freedom from this right now it's crazy. Of course I am still working on it every day because we should never stop growing, and we all have days that challenge us more than others. Check this out, though: if you really stepped back and thought about how much fear plays a part in your life, you might just shout, "Whoa!"

Fear of failure, fear of not being good enough, fear of not being good-looking enough, fear that you are just average, fear that no one loves you, fear of not knowing who you are and what you are doing here, fear of your parents divorcing, fear of a breakup, fear of how drugs are gonna destroy you, fear of not being saved, fear of not going to heaven, fear of not making the right choices, fear of saying the wrong things, fear of a boring life, fear of not knowing, fear of no one actually seeing you for you—fear is an unpleasant emotion caused by the belief that someone or something is dangerous, likely to cause pain, or a threat.

Did you catch that? Fear is just an emotion. It is completely in the mind and cannot have any part in your life unless you let it. It's a feeling that can lead to destruction if not handled properly. Fear isn't even a thing unless you let it be a thing. We can think about something so much that we can become that thought. So if we think about things that make us feel afraid, we will become afraid. We need to commit to start thinking and speaking things into our lives that counter fear. "I will no longer feel this way or think that way," "I am not a victim; I am a victor!" "I shall overcome." You and I do not have to think about what we don't want to think about. Fear, in essence, is a choice. So why choose fear? It literally doesn't have to be part of our lives. I choose not to worry.

Choose to tell yourself how much you trust God today. The more you tell yourself positive things about how God is in control, you will live it, be it, and feel it. I say we choose the power of the Holy Spirit over an emotion that clouds our true selves.

Do you realize who you have at your back, at your side, and in you? God! I will not fear because I got Jesus, baby! Paul the apostle said, "To live is Christ and to die is gain." That verse is my life verse. It's part of my code. My life is God's anyway, so whatever He chooses to do with it, awesome! I will live for Him while I am here with reckless abandon, and when I get to heaven, Jesus and I can hang out and sing Bob Marley songs and surf forever. At least that would be pretty cool. It shocked me once I realized fear isn't even a thing. So I was literally defeating myself by thinking negative, fearful thoughts. You and I have got to get in the habit of overcoming our minds so that our lives begin to play out those overcoming thoughts. If you are a negative thinker, you will live a negative life. When you speak life and think positively, you feel like Superman…without the tights and flying ability.

You will absolutely face adversity in this life. If not today, then tomorrow or the next day. It's a big part of this crazy life, and I'm saying let's use it to our advantage. There are so many teachable moments we miss in life, especially when we are growing up. Remember, just because you failed at something doesn't make you a failure. It is just an opportunity to learn and become incredible. So fail and fail often if that's what it takes to get awesome at your craft. Whatever you do, do not give up, because success is right on the other side of failure, and it could be the next attempt that changes everything. It's all in the mind and your outlook on things. Problems are just opportunities! When you go through life as an overcomer, you realize that what matters is you knowing you did your best. Some people spend their lives barely trying on the off chance they fail and then feel bad about themselves. Yet while they are doing this, they don't realize their self-esteem is getting destroyed. They could have been incredible had they put in the time and effort, maybe even pain, to get where they could have been.

If you are constantly worried about losing...you will lose. Worry is the opposite of trust. Trust in God, and there is so much more peace. Do everything you can, and trust in God that the outcome will be the best for you! Remember, God knows what you need to learn in order to become and do what He has called you to do. Accept that there are lessons to learn, and be mature about it. Thank You, God, for showing me that I didn't need that at this time or that this would have been bad for me. Thank You, God, for saving us from ourselves. We trust in You and know Your plan is better than ours. We are fighters, and we will not stop...ever! We are Yours and know that the King is coming, so we will work hard, play hard, and pray harder. There is no quit in us because You haven't quit on us.

What is your greatest fear? Perhaps you'll have to dig deep to really think about this; it may even be a fear that no one else in your life knows about. Why are you afraid?

Does fear hold you back from stepping outside your comfort zone? Why or why not?

What are some things you can do immediately to start changing your mind-set and become a fighter?

# From Fear to Faith Personal Testimony 3
# Ray Streets: Pastor– The Journey Church

Hello there. I'm so glad you are on this journey with Josh and Chad. When Josh told me about this book I thought "What a great idea." I am a reader, always have been and always will be. I can't remember a time when I didn't read…comic books, Hardy Boys, novels, biographies, etc. I love reading. I try to read at least one book a week and have done so for over forty years. That's a lot of books and a lot of reading.

So why am I so excited about this book? I was given a copy to read and asked for my opinion as well as any suggestions I might have. Then I was asked to contribute a story of my journey from fear to faith. I have been thinking a lot and praying about what I could share that would challenge you to step into faith and not be held in fear.

Like many of you I lived in fear. My biggest fear was that I wouldn't be liked and accepted. You would find that really strange if you knew me. You see I was popular, had many friends, and I was considered to be a great athlete( my opinion.)And being a good athlete was really an integral part of who I thought I was. I excelled in playing my favorite sport, basketball. I received a lot of honors, had many records, and was given a full scholarship to a Division 1 school.

That school is really where the fear overwhelmed me. Going to college and finding out that I might not be good enough really rocked my world. I was far from home and with people I hardly knew. I wanted, no, I craved acceptance.

This led me spiraling down a path that I was unfamiliar with. I turned to alcohol and eventually some drug use. This gave me the confidence I needed. But the reality was I was becoming someone I didn't know or like. I was in bondage and was no longer free. It was during this time in my life that I met a girl who I thought was my soul mate. Together we traveled this path of darkness and despair.

As we journeyed down this path I found myself more miserable than I had ever been. I couldn't go on living this life or this lie. I needed to be set free. Maybe you can identify and you're feeling much the same way. Well, I have good news! No, I have great news for you. Stop looking to the world for the peace you're missing. The world does not have the answer you are seeking. Jesus is the answer.

This is where I went from fear to faith. I recognized I needed to change. For me it was all about surrender, about not giving in to the world, but giving my life over to Jesus.

You see I failed to mention I had given my life to Jesus when I was young, but I really hadn't followed Him. I went my own way. As long as things went the way I wanted I didn't really need Him. But now I did and He was there waiting. I knew I had to leave that life and that meant changing playgrounds and playmates.

The first thing I did was ending the relationship with my "soul mate." I thought she was the one, but I knew God needed to be my soul mate and He needed to be first in my life. So I surrendered everything to Him. That took faith! There is a verse in the Bible that says, "Without faith it is impossible to please Him (God)."

Eventually as I traveled this new path of faith I began to have a peace and confidence like never before. Remember that girl who I thought was my soul mate? Well, she noticed the change in my life and she too gave her life to Jesus. We have now been married 44 years. It all began with that one small step of faith.

What are you holding onto that keeps you living in fear? God won't ask you to give something up to Him but that He will have something better to replace it with. You cannot out give God!

*Day 25*

---

# Move! Do Something! Be Radical!

**You will receive power when the Spirit comes on you, and you will be my witness.**

**-ACTS 1:8**

*Most of us aren't in danger of ruining our lives, we're in danger of wasting our lives.*

STEVEN FURTICK, AUTHOR OF GREATER

*Small dreams turn into incredible adventure.*

FROM MY SON ELI'S T-SHIRT

I remember as a kid my brother and I watching the movie *Aspen Extreme*. Most of you have probably never seen it, so I will give you a quick rundown of it, and yes, this has a point. The movie starts out with two best friends talking about how their lives are going nowhere. Here they are working for an automobile plant in Michigan, dreaming of a life of being ski instructors in Colorado. It was all just talk until one of them says, "Hey, let's do it." Next thing you know, they are packing up their van and heading toward Aspen. Living out and chasing after their dreams. I tell you all that because that is my first recollection of seeing people living out their dreams, and it started a passion within my brother and me for adventure. That movie struck a chord in our hearts that we are meant to live radical lives. Now when we have ideas, we go for it. It doesn't always make sense or turn out the best, but we try. Instead of just sitting around saying, "Maybe when I am older I will do something," do something today. Take a risk, do something out of your comfort zone. Maybe it's time for you to be a little radical.

I will never forget that probably one of the craziest things Trav and I did was right after I graduated college. I had always had a dream to travel the country. Some things had fallen through in my life, and I was kind of feeling down on life. I started talking to Trav about how cool it would be one day to just go—go see the country and explore new places. So that day we did exactly that. It might sound nuts, but we loaded up my Expedition and just drove. We called it our Walmart America tour, figuring if nothing else we'd sleep in parking lots along the way. We didn't set out a schedule or even know where we were going each day. We just woke up each morning, looked at a map, picked a place that sounded awesome, and went. In twenty-seven days, we covered 9,400 miles and made a figure eight of the entire country. We camped out in the Rockies, saw the sunset on the West Coast, drove through a redwood tree, were chased by buffaloes in Yellowstone Park, went snowboarding on a glacier, and even got to take in the wonder of the Grand Canyon. This trip truly drove my mom nuts because she never knew where we would be, but it is something that he and I will never forget. Why? Because we took a chance, we got off the couch, and we did something radical.

What is it for you? Throughout this whole book, we have been telling you about your faith. About who God is and who you are. We have talked to you about reading Scripture, about prayer, about conquering your fears, and about many other things. I say all this now because I want you to piece it all together. Think of it this way, like your life is a big puzzle, and all these chapters have been the pieces. You have the great designer Himself living within you and challenging you. God himself is holding the box to the puzzle called your life. It is now time to build your masterpiece. Or you can let it sit there...your move.

What is your dream? To see your school changed? Get up from your seat at lunch and go sit with the outcasts; it may turn into friendships you never expected. It may lead others to do the same. How about this thought even: start asking your teachers and others in school how you can pray for them. What a concept,

Christians praying for one another and trusting that God is going to do incredible things in your school.

How about your neighborhood? If you want to see hope in your area, then be that example of hope. Start praying for it. Do a prayer walk. Take some time to get to know your neighbors, maybe bake some cookies for them or take a meal to them. It may sound small, but I can promise you from my own personal experience the difference it can make. Three months ago I started walking our little area of Johnstown, praying for opportunities and passing out meals once a week. Within this time frame, I have started seeing the attitude of the neighborhood slowly change, and I even had the privilege of baptizing two of the men living by us. It is not that I am doing anything off-the-wall or crazy; I am just getting out.

In the movie *Evan Almighty*, Steve Carell, playing the role of Noah, asks God, "How do I change my world?" God replied, "One act of random kindness at a time."

Maybe that is all you need to hear right now to start taking action. Will you look back on your life and think about all the things you saw God do through you because you took risks? Or look back going, "Man, I wish I had taken a chance." If you are in school right now, that is the greatest mission field you will ever experience. If you are at work, you will reach others who Chad and I will never have a chance to reach. God has placed you where you are for a reason—to do something. No, wait, let me take that back. God placed to you there to change your world, to do something radical! It may seem like something small, or just a little vision, but God can take that tiny spark and turn it into a bonfire. Please, I am begging with you now, pleading with you through these pages, *live*. Will you start today?

Are you the type to take risks, or do you say, "Maybe when I am older"?

What if you are the one who God is calling to change your world?

Do you believe that God can take your tiny spark and set it ablaze? What would that look like for you?

# Day 26

## Return

*You have forsaken the love you had at first.*
*Consider how far you have fallen.*

REVELATION 2:4

Hello! I am fired up for this day, so I hope you are ready. I want to start out by painting a picture in your mind because it is the best way I know to relate this passage. Take a journey with me. Think about a relationship that stands out in your life. You were so excited about it. Think about that moment when you first locked eyes. You couldn't wait to talk to that person and get to know him or her more and more. You would stay up all hours of the night talking with such excitement, saying things like "No, you hang up first." Every detail about the person brought you such joy. You'd blush at the mention of his or her name. You had to tell everyone around you about this person, and others couldn't shut you up.

But then as time went on, that excitement started to fade, and the joy just wasn't there anymore. Talking on the phone became more of a chore than something you looked forward to.

What happened?

Life! Life happened!

I believe that is what the author, John, is explaining here in Revelations. The Ephesian church started out with such an excitement and passion for Jesus that they seemed like they could storm the gates of hell, and face the crazy insane persecutions of Nero, and nothing would stop them. They had ministries going like crazy, and Paul even spoke of them as being the example to follow. In AD 60 Paul is commending them for the church they are and their zeal for Jesus. By AD 90, as John is writing this, he is pretty much saying, "What happened? You have forsaken that first love."

I would be naive in writing this to think that the entire way through this book you have had such joy and excitement in reading that you couldn't wait until the next day's reading. I would be naive in thinking that the entire time through this journey of faith with us that you have had such passion for Jesus that you couldn't wait to tell others about Him. I would be naive in thinking that fear never overtook you while on this adventure. Maybe you started out reading this after a mission trip or a summer camp, where you had such passion and wanted your faith to grow, but then you got home and back into everyday routine, and it seems that love and joy you once had has faded. What happened? Life!

In my own personal journey, my wife could tell you I go through highs and lows also. After a week of speaking at camp, I am ready to take on our city—no, even beyond that, our world—with the name of Jesus. After a mission trip to Haiti, you will find me speaking to anyone who will listen, even preaching at statues in Central Park if need be. I am literally on fire. But then, to be honest, I have days when I am exhausted, I am beat up, and I feel like I have no energy at all, let alone a love for Jesus. I am fried. People will ask me to go visit them in the hospital, and truly, it is the last thing I want to do. I have lost that zeal and first love. It happens!

For some of you, as you read this, you know exactly what I am talking about. It is the ministry that at one point you were so excited about starting or being part of, but now it is a chore. You used to have so much excitement and couldn't wait to go to church to meet others and be part of a community, and now it is just part of your weekly schedule. See what I am getting at here? Let me give you a diagnosis if this describes you: you have forsaken your first love!

Now I get super passionate about this, and I wish you could hear me through the page as I am now screaming at you, pleading with you, to return! Return to that moment of first love. Remember what Jesus did for you on that cross. The price He paid in offering you forgiveness. The extent He went to in taking the thorns to show you the love He has for you. Does it bring you to tears; does it move within you? Please take a moment right now and remember: return. Jesus doesn't want to be an afterthought in your life or just a blah spot. He wants to be a fire burning within. His spirit on fire, shining through. A light for others to see.

*He will baptize you with the Holy Spirit and Fire* (Matthew 3:11).
*You are the light of the world* (Matthew 5:14).

See the theme: be a light, shine, a passion burning within. Is that how you would describe your spiritual life right now? What is holding you back? To take chances and risks for Jesus, this will be key to continue returning to this spot in your life where Jesus is that first love. We want to see you skydive.

How have you forsaken your first love?

What steps will you take in returning to that spot?

In what ways does it bring you joy in doing God's work?

*Day 27*

# Never Alone

*Even though I walk through the valley of the shadow of death, I will fear no evil, for you are with me; your rod and your staff, they comfort me.*

PSALM 23:4

If you have ever heard me speak, you probably have noticed the tattoo on my chest. It means a lot to me, so much so that it makes me pause when I think about it. It says, "Never Alone," with a rugged wooden cross in the middle. There have been multiple times in my life when I thought I would end it all. Please understand that I am not glorifying suicide or depression or any of the things that could enter your mind when I mention this. This is simply part of my story, and we all have one to tell. You may be much stronger than me, with a mind that is unshakeable. My mind was cloudy, distorted, unhealthy, constantly moving, and I couldn't deal with it.

Imagine if you were on a boat and you went scuba diving in the middle of the ocean. You jump in, and before long you unintentionally swim away from your dive buddies. You are so far away from the boat, from your reference point, and you are alone. There is no boat in the distance, and no one can hear you yelling for help. You have watched so many movies you know you shouldn't panic, but it's hard not to let fear set in, and you begin to stress out because of all the what ifs. What if no one finds me? What if this is it? What if they didn't even care enough to keep searching? What if I am completely *alone*?

You have no life preserver, so your arms and legs begin to get tired. You haven't prayed in a while, and truthfully, you never gave much to God but a few dinner prayers and church visits. There is only one hope. A miracle! You have almost no strength left, and your head begins to go underwater. You kick and kick, moving your arms until they are cramping up just to stay afloat. This is it! "God, forgive me for my sins," you cry out. "Jesus! Save me! I need you, and I am sorry for what I have done against you." You slowly start drinking more water in because your muscles give out. Your body completely gives out and, sinking, you give one last kick to keep your mouth above the water, and with your last breath, you scream, "You are Lord!"

Your face is completely submerged, but your foot hits something hard. As you're sinking you turn around and notice it's a rock underneath the water. You climb the rock, and right as your mouth gets above the water, you gasp for air. Ahhhhhhhh! After a couple of deep breaths, you turn around, and it's the most beautiful island you have ever seen. You didn't see it while you were freaking out in fear. You stand up and notice there is something written in the sand: "I'll never leave you." You fall to your knees and cry. There has never been a moment you have felt so loved. You also realize at that moment that God was there. All your feelings about God not loving you, not being there, and all the other excuses we come up with are gone!

This is how I have felt, and it is the best way I can describe my story with God. I started with people who love me and then got lost with people who didn't. I drifted in fear and anger while losing energy, identity, and the will to keep going. I hope you see that there is hope...always! While you have breath in your lungs, there is hope. We get so lazy and think there is all the time in the world to give our lives to Jesus until there isn't. We should live beyond the fear and laziness so that we can thrive and have peace in the midst of the craziest circumstances. You are never and will never be alone. You and I, for whatever reason, convince ourselves we are at times. Again, if God cannot lie and He says, "I am with you," why live as though God is a liar? God is always with you! You can't push God away, but you can walk away or run away. The problem with that is He will still be there, even if you don't want Him to be.

Eric Thomas says, "When you want to succeed as bad as you want to breathe then you'll be successful." I am telling you we need to want Jesus more than we want to breathe. Can you imagine how successful at living for and with Jesus we would be?

Maybe we aren't at that point yet, but let's make it a goal. If you feel alone or just plain bad today, tell yourself, "God is with me. I am not alone. Fear has no place in this moment. Anger has no place in my life in this moment. I am here to be a blessing, not to take other people's blessings. Not to bring people down because I feel a certain way. No longer will I live with an alone mentality; instead, I will live a life of vitality and victory."

If you are reading this and going through a serious case of depression or something that really has you down in a way you don't feel able to change, please talk to someone. Talk to your parents, a pastor, someone you trust and who is an authority figure in your life. God places people in our lives we can confide in and talk to in order to get direction when our minds are cloudy. Put people around you who share the idea that God is always with us. Friends who make you feel alone and drain you might not be the best of friends. Fear of not knowing that you can make other friends is common. You are not alone in this either. Yet if fear is an unpleasant emotion by definition, then let's realize that this fear is a feeling about an action that has not and probably will not take place. Tell yourself you can and you will put people in your life who fill you up, not drag you down. Think about three people who are this type of positive influence. Now find ways they can be a bigger part of your life. Ask them if you can hang out with them. Go to youth group with them. Find or start an activity with them. You are never alone. Jesus lives in you, so let His peace and presence be your guide, not worry and loneliness.

Do you often feel like you are alone? Explain.

How can you start living today with the knowledge that God is not a liar and that He is truly always with us?

Reach out to the three people you thought of above. Tell them how much they mean to you in this life, and ask them to continue being an even larger influence in your life. Ask them to help you live in Jesus's peace and presence. Write out here how you will do this.

*Day 28*

---

# Passionately Pursue Your Purpose

*Therefore, my dear friends, as you have always
obeyed—not only in my presence, but now
much more in my absence—continue to work
out your salvation with fear and trembling,
for it is God who works in you to will and
to act in order to fulfill his good purpose.*

PHILIPPIANS 2:12–13

*But if from there you seek the Lord your
God, you will find him if you seek him with
all your heart and with all your soul.*

DEUTERONOMY 4:29

So in this moment, I am currently listening to David Crowder... loud! One of the lines in his song says, "The cross meant to kill is my victory." God used a human device, the cross, meant for torturing people, to save mankind from themselves. I need to get out this point just in case you haven't thought about it in a while. God is so holy that even one sin separates us from Him. There is no one, ever, besides Jesus Christ, who has not sinned. God is perfect, and somehow we make ourselves out to be more than we are. We don't like knowing there is anything wrong with us but, y'all, we have a sin problem. What if Jesus hadn't died on the cross to rise again, defeating death? Our punishment should have been death and destruction.

You guys, it is hard for me to even write about this without crying at how amazing God is. Jesus thought of you on the cross, knowing you were going to mess up, turn against Him, walk away, and so on. The craziest things is that while He was feeling that pain, He looked to heaven and asked the Father to "forgive them." It is still hard for me to understand that kind of love and passion. As you read this, pause and think of how insanely cool this whole thing is. *You* are forgiven through the blood, death, and resurrection of the Holy One. Amazing! He lived His purpose on earth. It was to live a sinless life and then to die...for you! Then be resurrected from the dead. Satan, who is a punk, thought putting Jesus on the cross would end our hope. Guess what? Homey was wrong. Way wrong! Now through that gruesome death, hell is defeated.

Be obsessed with Jesus! Be obsessed with your purpose! You will have people tell you all this is crazy and you can't do it. Let the most powerful motivation come from those who say you can't do it. Don't get down, get prayed up! Don't let these distractions distract you. You and I have a purpose. Instead of dying on a cross like we should have for our sins, it is to die to ourselves. Our selfish desires get in the way of our pursuits. We think about ourselves so much that there are times we don't even recognize the person we are becoming. Get your mind off of you and onto Jesus. It is actually very simple, but it seems extremely difficult when you are constantly worrying about what everyone else thinks about you and what they are doing. How do I look more like them? What do they think about me? My question for you is: How can you get close to Jesus with the billion other people you have put in front of Him?

Prioritize things in your life. Maybe ask yourself what your priorities really are. What does your day look like, and is Jesus the one who is put in front of all of that? If you don't have a passion for Him, this is the reason. He might not be a priority, and maybe you just now recognized it. Change your mind-set. Do not feel bad; just realize the issue and quickly fix it. It's that simple. There might be times when we tremble in God's presence. It might be so amazing to be near Him that we are a little afraid of just how incredible He is. This is not like being afraid God will hurt you, but the majesty, the awesomeness of the moment is so big that we are humbled and have respect for how *big* our God is. Do not be afraid to fail. It's better to be in this than not at all, but you might as well give it your all.

What are you willing to die for? You want passion in your life? Be willing to give your life for Jesus. He gave His for you. Just that thought of knowing your life is in His hands gives us a sense of risking it all because He took it all for us. Pursue, seek, run after Jesus every day, and you will know your purpose.

Your main purpose is to bring glory to Him, and along the way those other questions you have will be answered. Don't waste the next breath now when your last one will be wanting Jesus anyway. In other words, don't let your last breath on this earth be the only one that wanted to give everything for Jesus. Live that way today.

Some people start drifting like a sailboat without its sail up, the whole time asking why the ship isn't moving faster and why it seems a little boring. They could have just looked up and noticed, "Oh, the sail isn't up." The only way for the boat to pick up speed and to head toward a destination is to have the sail catch the wind. Put up your sail (pursue Jesus), and let Him light that passionate fire in your life. Let Him be that wind in your sail that drives you and gives you the forward momentum to not give up and to not give in. The drive that makes you feel alive and that your life is about something bigger than yourself. The pursuit for your purpose that wakes you up in the morning to do a happy dance. It's OK to have happy feet for Jesus. Do a little dance, pray a little prayer, get up today! Good song. Work this thing out today and every other day. Prioritize so that the pursuit of Jesus becomes your passion. Oh man, that was good. You were meant for more, more than you could have ever imagined. Get up, wake up, pray up, and get filled up so that you can passionately pursue your purpose today.

*Life takes on meaning when you become motivated, set goals and charge after them in an unstoppable manner.*

—Les Brown

What is God's purpose for you on this earth? Why?

Do you believe that when you get close to Jesus He will guide you to the answers to your other questions? Why or why not?

What are some ways you can start your day being excited about why you exist? What are some things you can tell yourself to stay encouraged and inspired?

# Day 29

# You Want me to do What?

*Therefore go into all the world making disciples*

-MATTHEW 28:19

*Come, follow me and I will
make you fishers of men*

-MATTHEW 4:19

"I have no clue what inner-city ministry looks like. Why would you want me to go there?" That was my response when a friend of mine in college asked me to go to the projects with him one Saturday morning. Now, so you understand the complete picture, I was a scrawny little dude, and he was a tank of a man, so when he asked, I really didn't have much of an argument. It was one of those moments when you are trying to come up with every excuse in your mind but nodding your head yes because of the intimidation factor...so I went. And it was life-changing for me and started me on the path of life I still am on to this day.

We went into these projects, knocked on doors, and just invited kids out to throw a football around with us for a couple of hours. After that we had like a fifteen-minute devotional with them and snacks. Sounds simple, right? But my buddy that day said, "Josh, that is ministry. You built relationships." He went on to say, "Think about Jesus's ministry. He ate with people, He drank with people, He just spent time with them building relationships." The crazy thing about all this is that I was at Liberty for youth ministry but had missed this concept of simple one-on-one relationship ministry. It took me going to the projects, which I really didn't want to do, for God to get hold of my heart.

Fast-forward with me a few years. I had just finished college and was working at the local snowboard shop while at the same time doing an internship at a local church. As skater after snowboarder came through the doors of the shop, God started drawing my heart to outreach toward these kids, who had mostly been rejected by the church. I started praying for them and asking about how to share the Gospel with this "outcast crowd." God replied in His own way: "I gave you the example in building relationships. I made you to take the message of Jesus to them." Guess what? He told me to do the same thing that I learned in college, to go to them and to build relationships. A few weeks later, here we were at the local skate park with hot dogs and water, doing exactly what Jesus did. I wanted to use every excuse I could not to be there—"God, I don't skate. God, I'm not a good skater"— but God wasn't letting me just pray for these kids. He just kept saying, "If there is a need, then do something, anything." That ministry grew into having our own full-time indoor skate park in the area with thousands of kids coming through the door. "God, You want me to do what?"

One summer later I received a phone call that I still just laugh at and can't believe. Soulfest, a major Christian Music Festival in the Northeast with around twenty-five thousand attendees, heard about the skate park and asked us to bring our skate team up and do demos. I had no clue what that meant and honestly didn't have a skate team, but I just replied, "Sure, we will be there." I got off the phone and told my brother and my parents, and they just looked at me. In my mind I kept thinking it couldn't be that hard to figure out, right? We have skaters, they want a team, so let's make this work. What kid wouldn't want to travel to New Hampshire? So we called about five of the local guys and two friends from Colorado, and we told them about the opportunity. Needless to say, they were in. We got ourselves a skate team. Let me tell you, God was at work in ways I can't describe or even understand. Out of these skate teams, though, we got to go literally all over the country, ministering to thousands of youth along the way. I could have told them I didn't know what it meant to have a team, but I just trusted that God was calling us there, and out of it all, my world was forever changed. "God, You want me to do what?"

From the skate park came the church. Literally, we bought an old Catholic church. It was more the idea of wanting out of my parents' house, and the newspaper listed a crazy buy-one, get-one deal. You buy a house, you get a church with it. So, yeah, now that we had a church, God told me to start a service. So one Sunday night, a friend of mine showed up and asked what I was doing that week. At the time I was still single, so my plans were very flexible. Next thing I knew, he and I were on our way to LA, a thirty-six-hour drive. The key factor here, though, is he didn't tell me why we were going until we got about halfway into the trip. "By the way, we are going to work with the homeless on Skid Row." Yeah, that detail would have been nice to know...as I start going through all the preconceived judgments in my mind. Drug addicts, bums, lazy...and the list goes on.

That week my world was forever changed again. We met families there who truly were just down on their luck. One man, I will never forget, was a prominent architect until the financial crash happened. After that his wife left him and took the kids and the house. (Sounds like a good country song.) Anyway, after spending a week with these people, God broke Jeremy and me both. As we left that place, we couldn't even speak for the first few hours into the drive home, which is rare for us. Our prayer became, "If people like this exist in Johnstown, open my eyes." I promise you, to this day, I can't go by Central Park without seeing all those I had just ignored before.

Over the last ten years, I have seen God work in crazy ways time and again here in Johnstown, but probably one of the greatest ways is at a dinner my wife and I help serve on Thursday nights. It is a dinner for the "broken" (those just down on their luck, because the truth is we are all beggars sharing bread). From serving there we began to hear these men's and women's stories. She started hurting for them as she heard their needs beyond food. Hygiene products, pillows, blankets, all the stuff that we take for granted. So she started praying, "God, how can we take care of these issues?" He replied again (go figure), "I did. I made you." She came up with this plan to get local churches to partner in what she called Project Helpsome, collecting one item a month for an entire year. At the end of the year, we were able to package over one hundred bags filled with all these basic needs for members of the church to pass out locally, in Pittsburgh and in Baltimore, to the broken. Through this, again, it allowed us to build relationships. See the pattern yet? "God, You want me to do what?"

I could go on and on with examples of God moving here in Johnstown over situations like this. Somebody sees a need, they pray, God responds by saying, "I made you to meet that need," and out of it, ministry happens, relationships are built, and lives are changed.

I bring all this up on this day because I believe every single one of you who is reading this book has seen a need in your life that you wish God would do something about. Maybe it is reaching out to the outcast in school, maybe it is the family in your area in need, maybe it is the homeless or a ministry in the projects. I challenge you now to pray that God will open your eyes to where He wants you. It may mean you getting plugged into a local ministry that already exists that has been praying themselves for help, and you are going to be the answer to their prayers. Allow Him to lead you, and then watch where it goes. To finish off this day, I want to give you the lyrics from a Matthew West song, "Do Something," that rocked my world when it comes to this concept:

*So, I shook my fist at Heaven*
*Said, "God, why don't You do something?"*
*He said, "I did, I created you."*

What is it in your life that is breaking your heart? What is it that you want to see changed? The question then becomes: Does it break your heart enough that you will actually do something? God is calling us to be a generation of radicals who take His word seriously, to understand that we have the same spirit living within us that the disciples had when they shook the world, and to be bold. It's time to step up and go skydiving. I say that because, just like with skydiving, there will be fears, but our God is greater than your fears.

*For the Spirit God gave us does not make us timid, but gives*
*us power, love and self-discipline* (2 Timothy 1:7).

"God, You want me to do what?"

What are ways that pop into your mind that you can do something about the broken around you (sit with the outcasts in school, host a food drive, etc.)?

Have you ever looked at these opportunities as God wanting to work through you for a bigger purpose?

What if you, yes you, are the way God is trying to answer someone else's prayer? How does that make you feel?

*Day 30*

---

# Pick Your Head Up and
# Get Back in There

*Nothing in all creation will be able to separate
us from the love of God that is in Christ Jesus*

*-ROMANS 8:37-39*

It's crazy how life works sometimes. I was looking for the perfect
analogy to start closing out this book, and I knew I wanted to
speak on grace. I kept coming up with idea after idea, but none
of them really hit home like I wanted them to. Then God came
through like only He can. Two weeks ago my pops and I decided
to take a day off from everything and just go relax while watching
some Little League World Series games. What an experience; we

had a blast. We got there in time for the international game, with the winner going to the international championship. Turned out to be an awesome game, coming down to the final inning. What we were really there for was the US game, though. Talk about pressure; here these kids are ten to twelve years old, vying for a spot in the American Championship. ESPN is there, former pros are there, fans from around the country—yeah, this is a pretty big moment. In the top of the first inning, a kid hits a grounder right to the shortstop (who happens to be the captain of the team). A pretty routine play, but right as he goes to field it, it takes a bad hop, hits right off him, and goes into left field. You can tell by his reaction that he is visibly shaken by it. Two batters later, it's hit right at him again, a hard line drive; should be able to turn two and get out of the inning, but instead it goes off his glove, allowing a run to score. Before the inning is over, his team is down 8–0. As he is walking off the field, you see his head hanging, eyes looking straight down, trying to pull his hat over his face. The biggest moment of this kid's life, and he feels he let his team down. You can see his teammates trying to console him, and then his dad comes out of the dugout and puts his arm around him. I don't know what was said, but I can imagine. "Son, it happens. Life happens. You will fail at times. But now it is time to pick up your head and get back in the game." That kid could have quit, taken himself out of the game. His dad may have been a little disappointed. The truth is, though, that kid went on to crack a massive home run. His team would still end up losing, but I can almost guarantee you that going home he was going to remember the home run he hit at the Little League World Series! Not many people can say they have done that.

As I left that day, I started thinking about this series of events in light of my son, Eli. Would I love my son to grow up and never fail, never screw up, never miss a grounder, or never make an error per se? Absolutely. Will Lindsey and I have rules for him that he thinks are stupid, and he'll break them along the way? Without a doubt. Will he grow up and disappoint us at times, when we have to sit down and have a talk with him and maybe even discipline him? Surely. I would love to say no, but the only person who ever lived a perfect life was Jesus. It made me think back to when I was a kid and broke my parents' rules, and my dad would sit me down and say, "Josh, you really disappointed me on this one, buddy, and you know I am going to have to discipline you." In my mind I would be thinking, "Actually, Dad, you really don't need to take away the car if you don't want." Now I look back, though, and realize my parents' discipline was for my good so that I would learn that they wanted what was best for me. The other thing they always let me know was that no matter how much I would let them down, they still loved me.

I truly didn't understand the depth of it until Eli was born. He isn't even two years old yet, and already he will drive me nuts, disobey me, and make me want to pull my hair out. He will look Lindsey and me square in the eyes and say, "Um, no," defying us when we tell him it is time to come inside or to get down off of something. It is crazy to think as he gets older it is only going to get worse, but then I think about my own dumb decisions I made growing up. Yet in all Eli's mistakes and failures, there is absolutely nothing that is going to separate that love I have for him. He is my dearly loved child. Just like that dad whose son had an error playing baseball, he still loved his son. Same thing with my dad still loving me all the times I lied and tried to blame my younger brother.

Now think about this in the ways of God. In Christ, you are His adopted child, bought with a price, part of His family. If my earthly parenting love can never be separated for my child, how much greater is God's heavenly love for you? Instead of taking my word for it, let's look to the author of love Himself, the one with all authority, and see what He has to say. Paul writes this with inspiration from God about that love for you.

> *For I am convinced that neither death nor life, neither angels nor demons, neither the present nor the future, nor any powers, neither height nor depth, nor anything else in all creation, will be able to separate us from the love of God that is in Christ Jesus our Lord* (Romans 8:38–39).

OK, are you catching all that? Did you see where he said nothing can separate you? Nothing, nothing, nothing! So when you trip and fall, get back up, knowing Jesus is reaching down to you saying, "I still love you." When you feel like a failure and can't seem to do anything right, remember that Jesus still died for you and is trying to lift you back up. You may want to hang your head and question if God still loves you. Don't just take my word for it as a parent; take His word for it.

Think of it this way: I am a beach person and love sitting and watching the waves come in one after the next after the next. Never ending, never failing, never stopping. Continual, whether you are sitting there watching them or not. Some big waves, like up over your head. Some waves that you can hardly see but are always there. That is God's love—sometimes it shines through in your life undeniably, and other times you can hardly sense it. Just like the waves, it is always there, unchanging for you.

I wanted to write this day toward the end because I know there will be times as you go through the rest of your life and choose to take radical, crazy steps for Jesus that you might trip and fall. Get back up and pick up your head, knowing the truth that God still loves you. That is grace.

One final thing to remember, though, and I have learned this from watching Eli's favorite movie, *Cars,* way too many times: sometimes it takes us going through those broken moments, where we question if God can still love us, for us to hit our knees and truly seek Him instead of our own strengths. In the movie it took Lightning McQueen going through a traumatic life experience trapped in a small town to find out who he really was and ultimately what his life was all about. God doesn't want you to stay in that broken moment; He wants you to cry out to Him, like a small child grabbing at His pant leg. As a loving father, He will pick you up and get you back on this journey.

Describe a moment where you felt you failed God.

How did you feel about His love toward you during that time?

How grateful are you now, in this moment, knowing God loves you unconditionally?

How does Romans 6:1–2 tie in with this thought?

I will finish today with a quote from my dad's favorite author, Phillip Yancey: "There is nothing you can do to make God love you more, there is nothing you can do to make God love you less."

## Day 31

---

# Skyidiving with Jesus

*Peace I leave with you; my peace I give you. I
do not give to you as the world gives. Do not let
your hearts be troubled and do not be afraid.*

JOHN 14:27

You are here! This is the last day of this book but the first
day of a never-ending journey with Jesus! You are being
called right now to live a life of insane passion and dedication
to the person Jesus Christ. Life throws punches our way, and
we get caught with one on occasion. Do not let these punches
turn you away or shut you down. Let it wake you up so that
you can step up. Right now Hurricane Harvey is destroying
my hometown of Houston, Texas. Through all the devastation,

what we are watching is millions of people coming together to rise above their circumstances. This is a great example of how we should live anyway. With or without a hurricane. In the face of adversity, you show that you can rise above the difficulty. Listen, limits are just like fears; they are more often than not just an illusion.

When a group of people *decides* to rally around a cause, there is nothing that can stop them. Deciding, or choosing to choose, is a huge part of walking in faith. Don't sit back and let things happen. Make choices, and act on what's right. When we are passive and not willing to make a difference, the world is less strong. You and I are here making choices that send ripple effects throughout eternity. Not acting on what God lays on your heart usually ends with you or someone else hurting or not becoming the person you could be. People who shake up this world are focused on the mission. They are willing to do whatever it takes to reach their goals. Let's be like this right now. Decide to decide. You are ready. Keep moving forward. It's time to live this thing out and to be a world-changer. This means influence your home life, influence your school, influence your sports teams, or whomever you come in contact with. This is what being a leader is…influence. It starts with you! God made you so that you could be the change in the world. Skydiving with Jesus is about knowing that God has your back, no matter what. No more living in fear, because the God of the universe is directing your steps. You are now a warrior on God's team, and you cannot lose. No matter what, if you follow Jesus, you are now a winner and will spend eternity skydiving with the King.

*Every great dream begins with a dreamer. Always remember, you have within you the strength, the patience, and the passion to reach for the stars to change the world.*
—Harriet Tubman

When you skydive there is a moment in the plane when you have to look out the door and about fifteen thousand feet down. All you see is the ground and clouds. You hear loud noises, and in that moment, there is a fear factor that kicks in. You think you are about to get sucked right out the door before you are ready. Your adrenaline kicks in, and your heart starts to pound. The instructor for your tandem jump counts down from three—three...two...one—and then pushes himself and you out the door. There is a split second that is terrifying because you have no idea if you will ever see anything again. You level out and face toward the landscape of the earth, heading toward it at 120 miles per hour. In that moment you realize there was no point in being afraid. You are completely in the moment, so why pass it up? Why let fear run you, knowing you are not promised tomorrow, but you have this crazy moment? So you smile the entire way down with absolute bliss. It is like nothing you have ever experienced. You are completely free and happy in the midst of a crazy, abnormal moment.

*There is no passion to be found playing small—in settling for a life that is less than the one you are capable of living.*
—Nelson Mandela

You realize it's just you and God at that point, and there's nothing you can do except enjoy the ride. Thank You, God, for life, the experience, the clouds, the air...and for parachutes...LOL. The instructor pulls the cord, and your chute opens. Relief hits you, but it's even scarier because you see everything, and you are just hanging out in the air still thousands of feet from the ground. It hits you just then that it is fun because it's a little scary. The not knowing is OK with you because it makes you feel alive. Nothing and no one can take away this moment from you, so you decide to take it all in. You embrace certain feelings you had and just let go. Once your feet hit the ground, you immediately want to do it again. Live life this way. Have some fun with the thought that there will be scary moments, and you will walk right through them. Fear should not control you; you control it.

*But God doesn't call us to be comfortable. He calls us to trust Him so completely that we are unafraid to put ourselves in situations where we will be in trouble if He doesn't come through.*

—Francis Chan

Life is not about playing it safe. I know there are people who love you, care about you, and do not want to see you hurt. I do not either. That being said, living with Jesus for real takes trust. Living for Jesus is not easy. It can be dangerous, but in a way, it is like skydiving. You know that if you completely follow Him, you will have insanely awesome moments that in your flesh will make you so scared. At the same time, you smile and realize it will make you feel more alive than ever before. Your maximum joy is on the other side of your maximum fear. You can't skydive halfway, so don't live for Jesus halfway.

*Too many of us are not living our dreams because we are living our fears.*

—Les Brown

Once you jump, embrace the feelings, and let God show you peace and joy in the midst of abnormal situations. Sometimes as you are growing, you will just have to leap, and on the way, you will develop trust in the God you so want to serve. Bumps, bruises, and scars are all part of the mission. These things do not define us, but they can absolutely grow us. So go skydiving on a daily basis. Let God give you a nudge out of the plane and into the air. When you are free-falling with the King, that's when you truly start to live. What is He nudging you to do today…right now? Your life is His anyway, so give it up as a gift back to Him for all that He has done for you. Embrace what holds you back, lean forward, and find yourself in the arms (parachute) of the King.

How do you feel about going skydiving with Jesus (obeying Him) now?

What are you going to do now, and are you excited?

Write down your goals for the next month and for the next six months. What do you want to accomplish?

Who do you want to be? What do you want people to say about you when it's all said and done?

# Conclusion

This isn't the end! It is just the beginning. You have only begun to understand all that God has for you. Every moment is worth it; every breath is awesome. Life is precious! Breathe in, and breathe out. That's how long it could take before it's over, but in every single breath, there is an opportunity to live and to speak the name of Jesus. Skydiving with Jesus is about trusting God in all circumstances. When God lays something on your heart, go skydive with Him. Trust in Him, and let Him change you and your world one moment at a time. There are so many resources available to you that can help you and encourage you on this journey. Talk to your youth pastor, parents, or anyone else you trust. Don't be afraid to ask questions. Josh used to ask me the same question every day in college: "Hey, Chad, what's God teaching you today?" I almost lost my mind at first. Then it started to make sense. If there was a perfect question someone could ask me, that was it.

Josh and I are extremely grateful to have had this time with you. Feel free to contact us as well. We love to talk about God. We aren't the greatest in other conversations. People ask us about bills and mortgages, and our minds just go to surfing and snowboarding. There will be moments of doubt. Listen, Josh and I have these feelings as well, but we also have our families, mentors, and each other. We also surround ourselves with godly people to lift us up. Put people in your life to help you grow. Start leaning into Christ as He leans into you. If you want to invest in others, first invest in yourself by being consumed with your Savior. You can't take people where you have never been. So continue in this race, and finish strong. This race isn't about placing. It is about a man. A King! Our King! Jesus! Amen!

We love you guys! Now go and live!

*KID, YOU'LL MOVE MOUNTAINS!*
*So…Be your name Buxbaum or Bixby or Bray, or Mordecai Ali Van Allen O'Shea,*
*You're off to Great Places! Today is your day!*
*Your mountain is waiting, So…Get on your way!*
—Dr. Seuss, *Oh, the Places You'll Go!*